PRAISE FOR
WHAT THE ANIMALS TAUGHT ME

"In this deeply insightful book, Stephanie Marohn explores through each heartwarming story, the nature of our relationship with animals and the often unintentional harm we may inflict on some of those we believe we love. *What the Animals Taught Me* leads to important questions: How well do we communicate with animals in our care? How do we react when we see someone abusing a dog or a donkey? Marohn shares with us some of the profound lessons that she has learned from the many animals she has rescued."

—JANE GOODALL, PhD, DBE; founder of the Jane Goodall
Institute and UN Messenger of Peace; *www.janegoodall.org*

"*What the Animals Taught Me* recounts Marohn's inspirational personal journey. An illuminating account of her touching experiences with rescued animals, it describes the animals' deep inner lives and demonstrates how the connections we make with fellow animals can inspire and teach us about ourselves."

—GENE BAUR, founder of Farm Sanctuary and author of *Farm
Sanctuary: Changing Hearts and Minds about Animals and Food*

"*What the Animals Taught Me* is a heartwarming book that deserves a wide readership. Stephanie Marohn and her dedicated coworkers selflessly provide a safe haven for animals of all shapes and sizes— horses, deer, donkeys, sheep, chickens, and others—and has written inspiring stories about these amazing beings who owe their very lives to this amazing woman. I will never forget Pegasus the horse or a deer named Angel. Read their tales, weep with sadness and joy, and embrace the trust, loyalty, and love our furry and feathered friends offer to us."

—MARC BEKOFF, author of *The Emotional Lives of Animals, Wild
Justice: The Moral Lives of Animals,* and *The Animal Manifesto: Six
Reasons for Expanding our Compassion Footprint*

WHAT THE ANIMALS TAUGHT ME

Stories of Love and Healing from a Farm Animal Sanctuary

STEPHANIE MAROHN

HAMPTON ROADS

Cover design by Barbara Fisher / www.levanfisherdesign.com
Interior design by Maureen Forys, Happenstance Type-O-Rama

Photo credits:
Pegasus (p. 5) by Molly Munro.
The hens (p. 80), New life (p. 83), and In the bird yard (p. 85)
    by Marji Beach/Animal Place.
Sylphide and Ulysses (p. 174) by Regina Kretschmer.
All other photos are by the author.

Hampton Roads Publishing Company, Inc.
Charlottesville, VA 22906
Distributed by Red Wheel/Weiser, LLC
www.redwheelweiser.com

ISBN: 978-1-57174-657-3

Library of Congress Cataloging-in-Publication Data is available on request.

Printed on acid-free paper in the United States of America

MAL

10 9 8 7 6 5 4 3 2 1

To Charlotte, Wonder, and Gabriel
with all my love and deepest thanks

Contents

1

The Winged Horse

THE FIRST TO ARRIVE WAS A HORSE. I was gazing out the kitchen window in a dishwashing reverie one morning when a tiny mare, half the size of a regular horse, pranced into view. Pure white, with a long white mane and tail, she looked like a unicorn, minus the horn. I watched in wonderment as she tossed her head and danced away. Was she really there?

I got outside in time to see her trot up to the gate over which the two full-size horses who lived on the property were craning their necks, eyes wide at the sight of her. The visitor touched noses with the gray gelding. The chestnut mare next to him promptly bit the little one on the head. The white horse squealed and leapt back but wasn't truly perturbed. She was overflowing with the ecstasy of freedom.

I moved forward and she walked to meet me, nosed my outstretched hand, and gazed at me from jet-black eyes rimmed endearingly with long white eyelashes. The top of her head reached no higher than my chest. Later I learned that she is a miniature horse, which is bred differently from a pony. After greeting me, the little horse danced off again, back to the gate, where she got in another touch on the gelding's nose before ducking away from the mare's reach. Gabriel, the wild desert donkey, approached tentatively to see what the commotion was about. He was at the bottom of the herd's hierarchy (the mare was at the top), which meant he couldn't push into the others' space, so he hung back, but his eyes were riveted on the new arrival.

I watched the little white mare tossing her head and prancing before them. She held herself as if she had no weight, like a dancer does, which in equestrian circles is called "collection." The ability to do this is a regal trait of horses and it is thrilling to see. When horses are collected, they seem to float, their feet hardly touching the ground. They are complete grace and utterly, fully present.

How had this little horse gotten onto the property? The eight acres were fenced. But rather than question the marvelous gift, I went to fill a bucket of water for her.

That afternoon, a teenage girl came looking for the horse, who it turned out had broken her tether a few houses away. The little mare raised her head to look at the girl, but lowered it again to the bounty of the grass. We stood watching her graze and speculated about how she had ended up here. We concluded that someone must have come across her on the road, seen the sign on my driveway gate requesting those who entered to close the gate after them because horses were loose on the property, and figured this was where she belonged. Rural Sonoma County, where I live, still operates in the old farm way: passersby take responsibility if they see a cow, horse, sheep, goat, or pig loose and take the time to herd the animal to safety.

The little mare must have slipped her halter to get free of the tether because she was wearing no sign of ownership or bondage—a fairy horse, entirely her own being. That's the vision of her I still carry, and my memory blurs when I recall the girl putting a rope around the little one's neck and leading her away. With the deep connection I have to this horse now, I can't believe I let the girl take her with no discussion of other options, knowing she would end up back on a tether, with no horse companions. Horses are herd animals and they pine in loneliness when they are forced to live without other horses. I knew all this and I loved animals dearly, but at that time my heart would open only so far; my mind could still persuade me not to follow my heart's promptings. "Adopting a horse would tie you down," my mind told me. "You already have a cat and that's enough of a commitment. Better just to enjoy other people's animals." So I let the little white horse be led away.

I didn't think I would see her again. But one morning a few weeks later, when I sat down at my computer to write and looked out over the expanse of summer-golden grass that stretched from the windows before me to the neighboring field, there she was. Tethered in the field beyond the fence line, with about fifteen feet of rope tied to a stake, she could only go endlessly round in a circle. Tethering is a terrible thing to do to any animal. It alters their minds to have their world limited to what they can reach at the end of a rope, just as it would the mind of a human kept that way.

The horse was out there all day, and the next day too. On the third morning, I saw that she had knocked over her water bucket. As the day wore on, nobody came to refill it. I could stand it no longer. The girl had told me where she lived, and I walked down the street to talk to her and her mother. After the usual neighborly exchange of who has lived where and for how long, I broached the subject of the little horse, asking if they were looking for a good home for her, gently suggesting that she might be happier where she could roam free and be with other horses. The mother said they actually would like to find a new home for her, that they had thought they could set up a fence—she knew what horses needed (there was a touch of guilt in this and a need to explain that she was aware the tether was a bad idea)— but they only rented the place and had had work setbacks recently, so they couldn't afford it. When I asked where the horse had come from, the woman said that a guy who owed her husband money for work he had done for him hadn't been able to pay and had given the horse in lieu of payment.

Before I knew it, I was walking the horse out to the road and heading for home. Looking down at her, I couldn't stop smiling at the thought that I would be seeing this magical creature every day. She went willingly with me, stepping along patiently at my side on her pearly hooves. I assumed she was used to being led where humans chose to take her. Now, looking back, I think she knew there was a grander plan. At the time, I thought I was merely rescuing a horse. She knew better.

As soon as we were inside the driveway gate, I took off her halter and stood back. She gazed at me for a moment with those beautiful black eyes, then flew up the gravel drive, heading for the herd. My heart lifted at the sight of her set free. Her true name came to me then: Pegasus. Her old name didn't make it past the gate.

Pegasus's new home was eight acres of pasture and brush. I rented the house on the property, worked at home as a writer and editor, and took care of the owner's two horses and donkey. A "no-climb" fence, a sturdy wire-mesh and wood-post construction designed for the safety of livestock, ran around the perimeter of the property and sectioned off three pastures, with gates to separate animals as needed. I closed the gate between the new arrival and the others for a few days until I was sure the large horses wouldn't hurt her. I wasn't worried about Gabriel. It was clear from their exchanges through the fence that they were already friends.

Pegasus

I hadn't planned on being the guardian of large animals. I'd come into the role after a long process of settling down that had begun for me eight years before when I left the city for the country. I had lived in one city or another, mostly

San Francisco, for seventeen years when one day I could no longer stand the sound of footsteps overhead. Auspiciously, the mother of a friend of mine had an unoccupied house in the remote hills above the Russian River in Sonoma County, the land of vineyards and wineries north of San Francisco.

My plan was to spend a month finishing a novel I was writing. The house was a perfect writing retreat—quiet, isolated, with a gorgeous view of rolling hills and few houses in sight. The day after I moved in, a wild cat showed up. He was starving, rail-thin, and had the hunched look of illness. I had grown up with cats and dogs in my rural childhood in Ohio and Pennsylvania, loving them ardently, but as an adult I also loved to travel and was reluctant to be tied down. I couldn't deny an animal in need, though. Within three days, the cat was sleeping in my bed. Recovery of his health took longer, but together we managed it. When I moved a year later to the eight-acre property where Pegasus arrived, the once-wild cat, now named Pooka, went with me.

The two horses who lived on this property were well-trained elders. That was a good thing because I had little experience with horses. They took a halter and submitted with no fuss to hoof trimmings and whatever veterinary care they needed; they just wanted to graze and be left alone. Donkeys are known as easy keepers, so Gabriel didn't require much either, at least at first. With Pegasus's arrival, I was introduced to all my shortcomings.

I let her run free, which was fine as long as I didn't need her to do anything, but then she stopped taking the halter and would run away when I approached her to put it on. I had no idea what to do. I was aware that an experienced horsewoman could solve this problem in two seconds, but I didn't have those skills. What I did have was an innate connection with animals and a belief in the path of love to achieve cooperation. I was sure we could work this out, and when she tossed her head and took off to avoid the halter, I had enough sense to see that it was my failing, not hers.

There is nothing quite like the proving ground of the pasture. You can't hide inadequacy out there. And since I lived alone, the responsibility fell entirely on me. Butterflies of anxiety fluttered in my stomach. I was afraid of doing it all wrong, and worried that in my ignorance I might cause Pegasus some psychological damage, though all I was doing was following her around with the halter.

One night I went out to round her up because I was leaving the next morning for a week and didn't want her loose on the property without me there. Like the tyro I was, I waited until late at night to do this. An experienced horse person wouldn't wait until after dark, much less ten p.m., and would have established a routine of roundup around dinnertime. I had always hated schedules and hadn't yet learned that everything goes much easier with animals when there is a consistent routine. In avoidance of the halter confrontation, I had been hoping Pegasus would put herself to bed. Sometimes she did.

Pegasus and helper

By the time I went outside, it was stormy. Wind tends to make horses wild. Again, at the first sign of a pending storm, a pasture veteran would have rounded her up immediately.

But there I was, walking the fields in the rainy dark, calling her name, which was more for me than for her. The wind took my voice, and it was unlikely that she would have come even if she had heard—free life was way more compelling at that point. I was thoroughly soaked when I finally saw her ghostly white form in the lower field, not far from the house. Rain and wind whipped around us as I approached. When she turned to look at me, her eyes were wild, the whites showing. When I tried to put on the halter, she wheeled and kicked up her heels, catching me on one thigh, and then raced off into the dark.

I didn't think she had aimed for me; the wheeling and kicking was her dramatic exit. I burst into tears, not so much because it hurt, though it did (a hefty bruise would serve for weeks as a reminder of just where ignorance can get you), but out of frustration and an overwhelming sense of failure. What did I think I was doing? I didn't know anything about horses. I was probably making all kinds of other mistakes in the way I was taking care of her. What kind of rescue was this—deliverance from a tether into the hands of someone who didn't know what the hell she was doing?

I stood there in the dark field in the rain and wind and cried. Suddenly, Pegasus was there, nudging at my arm. I stroked her neck and apologized through my tears for inflicting my lack of experience on her. She nudged me again and I realized she was inviting me to put the halter on her. She stood patiently while I did and then docilely allowed me to lead her to the other animals. It was obvious that Pegasus was comforting me, and she was willing to put aside her wildness to do it. I was in awe of the largeness of this little horse's heart.

In the synchrony of the universe, a woman who works with horses contacted me not long after that night about doing some editing for her. Christine's approach with horses fit my belief system (inexperienced as I was, I had a belief system). Rather than using equipment (halters and ropes) and training the horse to bow to the human's wishes, her focus is on horse and person establishing a relationship through companion walking without equipment. This is known as liberty work, or liberty training. We agreed on a trade of our skills.

Christine is a lifetime horsewoman who, after discovering the companion way, regretted her earlier unquestioning acceptance of conventional methods of training horses. Being a no-nonsense cowgirl, however, she didn't spend time bemoaning the fact, instead concentrating on becoming ever better at the companion work and expanding it into her own approach to the human-horse relationship.

Pegasus and me

As Pegasus and I walked side by side in the pasture during our first session with Christine, Pegasus kept turning her head to me, wanting to interact, touch, nestle. We were supposed to walk, eyes ahead but being watchful of each other out of the sides of our eyes as horses do, and match our pace. I had to keep gently pushing Pegasus's head away. When we walked for a time as we were supposed to, Christine instructed me to stop and give her a reward. First it was a bit of carrot or apple, but Pegasus glowed when I touched her, so from then on, the reward was a hug, a pat, or a rub.

After brief observation of us together, Christine informed me that she could see an unusually strong connection between us, but Pegasus was in charge. I didn't need an expert to tell me that Pegasus had me wrapped around her pearly little hoof. Whereas some people tend to project an ulterior or manipulative motivation onto a horse behaving in this way, Christine said simply that for the safety of the herd someone has to be in charge; since I hadn't taken the lead in our interactions, Pegasus had stepped into the void. (In the herd as it was forming on this property, the chestnut mare was the lead, but, for my own safety, I was supposed to be the leader of them all.) Pegasus had no ego attachment or investment in being the leader. This wasn't a power struggle. It was simply the way it was: someone needed to lead. I learned that the main way I was communicating my non-leadership to Pegasus was by walking in front of her or at her head instead of at her shoulder or slightly behind it. Contrary to the human way, the one in front is not the leader. The leader chooses the direction of movement and impels the other forward from behind. This is horse 101.

Another way I was signaling non-leadership was by allowing Pegasus to move me off my position. No horse in the herd moves the lead mare from where she stands (and no horse in the herd would kick the lead mare, even by accident!). Christine used an incident with a plastic bucket as a demonstration of this. Pegasus and I had progressed in our companion walking to navigating an obstacle course side by side. This was also to make it more interesting since we had both gotten bored with just walking around the pasture. We were weaving our way through the assortment of farm objects I had used to create the obstacle course, from a rusty wheelbarrow to a toolbox to a wooden crate to an empty industrial plastic paint bucket. Suddenly, a gust of wind whipped a tarp around the side of the barn and Pegasus spooked. She wheeled and took off, charging over the plastic bucket and shattering it.

"If you aren't the leader, you could be that bucket," said Christine. She explained that even when horses spook, they never invade the lead mare's space. They may turn and run in panic, but they automatically veer around the lead mare if she is in their path. For their own safety, people, being so outsized by horses in most cases, need to establish themselves as leaders. It's important even with horses the size of Pegasus, Christine continued, because if in her panic to escape the scary tarp she had run into me instead of the bucket, she could have really hurt me. I looked at Pegasus, now happily grazing, and was glad I was learning the Way of the Horse with a miniature. I had new appreciation for a friend of mine who works with stallions.

In one of our walking sessions, Christine handed me a riding crop, which had a leather cord attached to it. It looked like a whip and I hated it on sight. She assured me that I would only be using it like a tail. Since I don't have a tail and tails are an essential part of horse language, I needed some equipment to be able to communicate.

Pegasus and I walked around the pasture again, me holding the crop down at my side, the cord end behind me. When her attention wandered, I flicked my "tail" at her flank as the lead mare would do if a horse were dawdling or otherwise in need of direction. I did it only a few times and then stood still. Christine asked what I was doing; it took me a moment to answer because I was trying not to cry.

"I can't use this thing," I said finally, and burst into tears. I dropped the crop in the grass and moved away from it. I couldn't even stand to be near it. Pegasus, who had taken the opportunity to graze, came over then and gently nuzzled me, as she had when I was crying on that rainy night.

What was going on here? First, the crop was made of leather, which I avoided in clothes and animal equipment such as halters, using nylon or rope halters instead. I didn't want to use around the animals any products made from another animal's skin—what kind of message did that send? But second, what had really brought the tears was that the crop seemed to hold all the dark energy from the centuries of use of crops as a means to inflict pain on horses. I couldn't bear to walk at the side of my precious, pure-hearted horse and flick her with it. Though it didn't hurt her, it still felt like a violation. I knew I would never do it again.

"Okay, we'll come up with something else," said Christine matter-of-factly when I told her this.

I appreciated her accepting my very un-cowgirl-like behavior. I guessed we were in the process of reinventing what it means to be a cowgirl.

After that, I used a stalk of pampas grass. It felt clean in my hand and its plume was far more like a horse's tail anyway. But even that I didn't use for long. Pegasus got my messages, tail or no tail, and I didn't like flicking her with anything. I ought to be able to communicate in a more sophisticated way with her, I thought. And it was true. We began to develop a telepathic relationship, and the stalk of pampas grass only brought us back to a coarser form of communication.

The muse

We continued our sessions with Christine, though Pegasus had turned over the leadership to me after the first session and easily took the halter from then on. I saw clearly how my halter difficulties had been a communication issue. When I learned how to speak her language, even rudimentarily, the problem evaporated. My instinct had proven right. Exerting control is not the path to harmony. There is another way.

UNCONDITIONAL LOVE LESSON #1:
Letting Go of Control

IT WAS TWELVE YEARS AGO THAT PEGASUS began my training in the Way of the Horse and she is still my daily companion on that path. With her, I have learned how to walk the line between confidence and dominance. Like many animal lovers, I had always been reluctant to exert my wishes on the animals under my care. *Who am I to decide what they need to do?* I would say. You might be able to get away with that approach when it comes to a cat or a small dog. So the cat gets up on the table. So the dog doesn't always come right away when called. No big deal when safety isn't involved. But out in the pasture, with large animals who can hurt you, unintentionally or not, you have to step firmly into the leadership role.

With animals, what I had to learn was the difference between domination and wise guidance so I could be comfortable stepping up to the leadership plate. With Pegasus, I discovered that truly wise leadership operates through cooperation and harmony. Over time, I deepened my ability to create this with all the animals in my care.

Sadly, the concept of leading through cooperation and harmony is rare in the equestrian world. Many horse people are all about dominance and rule when it comes to their horses. Recently, I was walking with a friend on a forest trail when a woman in the saddle on an obviously distressed horse came down the trail toward us. The horse was wide-eyed, neighing, dancing sideways, turning, and otherwise attempting to escape the tightly reined-in hold the rider was trying to maintain. As they passed us, the rider whipped the horse's neck with a riding crop. I have always hated cruelty toward animals, and seeing it can send me into fierce rage.

In past years, before the animals opened my heart to all beings, I would probably have yelled at the woman, hotly berating her for her abusive treatment of the horse. In my righteous anger, I failed to see the irony of such a reaction—a person mistreating an animal, me mistreating that person. My heart was as closed to the person as the person's was to the animal. In my deep upset over abuse of animals, I withdrew all caring for the human involved. I didn't feel such a person deserved to be treated with respect.

But it was different on the trail that day. As the rider passed us, I sent love to the mare with the fervent prayer that the situation would change for her. I also sent love to the rider because I knew she was the one who needed to change. I have the animals to thank for this being my first and instinctual response. I had fully taken in what they had taught me about unconditional love.

Then the rider pulled the horse up just past us, forced the horse around, and struggled to keep her in place.

I approached slowly and asked if I could greet the horse. She nodded and I put a hand out to the mare. The mare was too agitated to interact and I could see her anxiety rising. She was nearly out of her head with it.

I began to talk quietly with the woman. In the conversation that followed, she expressed her frustration that the mare just wanted to get back to the barn and her herd and that she often resisted the woman's commands. The woman was forcing the horse to stand facing back up the trail. She was determined that the horse would give in and relax before she turned her around and let her head for home. There was no way that horse was going to relax under all that anger flowing from the person astride her.

I could see the situation was escalating as the angry rider continued to try to regain control and the horse became more upset.

"If you don't mind me asking, what's your ultimate goal here?" I inquired, keeping my voice calm with no note of criticism.

"I win, win, win," she said, without hesitation.

And there is the problem, I thought. But I said, "Have you considered that cooperation might be a better basis for a relationship?"

The woman must have taken that in some, because when I suggested that the situation might change if she dismounted and helped the mare calm down, she did. I was thinking how awful it must be for a horse to have on her back a rider whose motivation is to win, win, win, with no thought of what is good for the horse or how distressing that angry, controlling energy must feel coming through the saddle, the stirrups, the reins, and the riding crop into the horse's body with no means for the horse to escape it aside from throwing the rider. The horse either cared enough about her rider not to do that or had been severely punished for it in the past.

When the woman dismounted, I saw the utter relief in the horse's body. She began to calm immediately. Soon the woman allowed the horse to turn for the walk back to the barn.

Before the woman went, I thanked her for letting me talk with her. I was truly grateful for how open she had been. She didn't know me, but yet she had been willing to listen, even in her own obvious distress. I think she was willing to listen to me because I approached her with caring and compassion, rather than with the need to teach her or berate her. What I felt toward her was real and she could feel it; it wouldn't have worked if I had had rage in my heart, but I had put on a show of compassion. I wanted her to stop sending all that angry energy into the horse, but it would work no better with her than with the horse to get angry and yell at her, be fakely nice, or otherwise alienate her with attempts at control. I had to try to elicit her cooperation.

I succeeded to a point, but that woman and her horse stayed on my mind for the rest of that day and days afterward. I thought of all that I could have said, should have said to help her see another way of being with her horse.

This is what I wish I had said: Can any relationship with anybody—animal or human—work when the motivation of one of the members in the relationship is to win, win, win? That motivation is all about controlling the other, rather than considering what is in the other's best interests. How can we feel good about a relationship when we know that the other just wants to win? That kind of win means someone has to lose. For a relationship to thrive, there must be a way for both members to win. And that winning can simply be defined as having found a way to work beautifully together. Cooperation and harmony, not control, is the motivation and the goal.

As I see it, humans' attempts to control arise out of fear and pain or, more accurately, the desire to keep from feeling fear and pain. In the case of the rider on the trail, perhaps she did not know how afraid she was, trying and failing to control this large animal. Anger often covers fear. But the attempt to control another only makes us feel worse, as it further closes our hearts. To open our hearts, we must let go of control, of trying to control others and our circumstances. When we do this, we have taken the first step toward being able to love unconditionally, the ultimate in harmonious relationships. When we love unconditionally, everything just works better.

Loving unconditionally doesn't mean, however, that we have no requirements in our relationships. I needed Pegasus to accept the halter so I could maintain her safety and her health. I needed to find another way besides force to reach that goal. Eliciting her cooperation by learning to speak her language, being clear in my objectives, and coming from a place of love and an open heart was that way. Getting angry at her seeming lack of acquiescence would only have entrenched us in a negative cycle that would have closed both our hearts and created years of problems (the woman on the trail was in such a negative cycle with her horse). At the same time, continuing to cry in the pasture, to fold before the task of building cooperation, would also have stalled (sorry!) our relationship.

Developing cooperation requires creativity. When I visited an animal sanctuary in New Zealand, I looked with wonder at all the animals accompanying the director and me as she showed me around—dogs, cats, chickens, baby goats, even rabbits. I asked how she had gotten the dogs not to chase the other animals. "I made what I was doing much more interesting," she said.

Developing cooperation requires more time than ruling by coercion does, but the rewards are great and ever expanding. You may be quickly able to bend an animal to your will using fear and force, but once you see what horses (or dogs or any other beings) who exist in cooperation with humans rather than under their dominion are like, you will never be tempted to go back to the old way of control. (And after my experience with the rider on the trail, I also can't imagine going back to my old way of raging at someone who is mistreating an animal.)

Letting go of the need to dominate allows trust and love to blossom. It is a basic lesson in learning to open the heart and love unconditionally. Loving unconditionally means we do not predicate our love on the other doing what we want. Loving unconditionally means we work together for the highest good of both of us. To enter the realm of unconditional love, we let go of our desire to control, and focus instead on our desire to connect and communicate. And soon, a whole field of flowers is blooming before us.

2

Wonder in Our Midst

EVERY DAY, PEGASUS AND I GREW MORE IN SYNC. I could feel the connection running between us, even from across the pasture. She and Gabriel had also become extremely close. Though Pegasus liked the horses, she spent her days side by side with the wild desert donkey. When the other horses moved away, six months after Pegasus arrived, she and Gabriel didn't seem to grieve. The horses' person, having seen what good friends the two were, left Gabriel for Pegasus. They were the only hoofed creatures on the eight acres then and they would often take off across the fields together, kicking up their heels and galloping in the sheer joy of open space.

We had a period of peace on the farm, and then something happened that had far-reaching effects—in more ways than one. I was going away again, this time for two weeks to visit family. Just before I got back, Pegasus got sick. The vet had only to see her walk to know what was wrong: founder. Dread word in the horse world. Miniature horses and ponies are particularly prone to this condition. Though the terms "founder" and "laminitis" are often used interchangeably, laminitis is actually the acute stage of inflammation in the tissue structures in the foot called laminae, whereas founder is when laminitis becomes chronic and the structure of the hoof is affected, sometimes to the point that the horse can no longer walk and has to be put down. One episode of laminitis makes it more likely to recur. The horse hobbles on stiff legs because the feet are so painful it hurts to walk. This was the way Pegasus was moving when I returned from my vacation. Rich spring grass can trigger laminitis, as can overeating and rich food in general. There are different theories as to why the rich food produces the hoof condition, but all agree that the animal must be pulled off the grass immediately, no matter what time of year it is. If laminitis goes untreated, the coffin bone inside the foot can actually rotate.

Horrified by that prospect, I determined to avoid it. The vet told me that Pegasus could not be let out to graze until the grass dried up in early June. It was the end of February. I couldn't bear the thought of keeping her in a small paddock for that long. "What if I kept the grass short in this area?" I asked, pointing to the pasture outside her paddock. I would mow it every week if I had to.

The vet looked the area over. "That would probably be all right," he said, adding, "You could get sheep to keep it down."

"How many sheep do you think it would take?"

"Two ewes ought to do it."

And what would the sheep need? Emus? This was way more than I had meant to get involved in, but what could I do? Pegasus needed sheep.

The next time I was in the feedstore, I asked Rae, the expert sheep woman who worked there, whether she knew of anyone who was looking for a home for two ewes. She sent me to Jane, who had two Columbian ewes.

"One of them has a lamb," said Jane on the phone. "Is that all right?"

I wouldn't have dreamt of separating a mother and child, but I was relieved to hear that the lamb was female. I wouldn't have to deal with the neutering issue.

I knew already that I was going to take the three sheep, but I arranged to go see them because that's what you're supposed to do in the practical as opposed to the magical world. Soon I was at Jane's ramshackle ranch (everyone I knew who had a farm or farm animals dreamt of the perfect barn and outbuildings, but none of us had them), looking over the fence at two large wooly white-faced sheep standing in a mound of straw in a small paddock. A lamb was curled up, barely visible, in the straw near them. The ewes eyed us warily and didn't approach. They didn't need to. We were already on a trajectory together.

In a nod to convention, I asked a few questions before arranging for Jane to bring the sheep to my place, which was only a few miles up the road. When Jane arrived in her pickup towing a U-haul-type trailer rigged with wooden slat sides, the sheep were baaing loudly and continually. She drove into the first pasture, by the barn, and we lifted off the trailer's rigged tailgate. The sheep backed up, huddling together. When we moved away, they made a mad dash for freedom, leaping out of the trailer. Then they ran all around, still baaing loud and long. I got a look at the lamb for the first time. She had a long tail. Jane explained that she hadn't gotten around to banding it when the lamb was little, and now she was three months old and it was too late. Banding involves placing a rubber-band-like device around the tail near the top to cut off circulation, which eventually causes the tail to atrophy and fall off. Sheep ranchers dock the tails to make shearing easier and, ostensibly, to help prevent parasites, but docking can actually increase the likelihood of parasites and cause other health problems.

Charlotte, Queenmere, and Chloe

Alert at the arrival of the truck, Pegasus and Gabriel approached, which heightened the sheep's agitation. But when Gabriel greeted them with the longest and most elaborate bray I had ever heard from him, the sheep stopped in mid-baa and listened. When he was finished, there was a moment of silence, presumably while they absorbed what he had said, and then they resumed their baaing.

After two days, adjustment and commentary complete, the baaing stopped. The sheep focused then on the abundant grass. After they ate the grass down short in the first pasture, I let them out on the rest of the property. It was an ideal place for sheep. They had acres to wander over at will, as much fresh grass as they could possibly want, and the presence of a donkey who is a natural protector against dogs and doglike animals like coyotes and wolves. Not that coyotes and wolves were a problem in my area, and the fences were secure against roaming dogs, but the sheep could relax their innate vigilance a little, knowing that a natural guardian accompanied them.

None of the sheep seemed to want to interact with me at first. I didn't take it personally. There was, after all, much to explore in their new world. They had never had so much space, with such a variety of vegetation. They had also never had a choice in their dealings with humans, so I let them go their own way. Within a week, the ewes baaed in greeting when I appeared and the lamb had begun happy pronging and sideways twisting leaps—a marvel to behold.

One morning, six weeks after the sheep arrived, I was woken from a deep sleep by a persistent sound close to the house. It took me a moment to come to full consciousness and realize that the sound was baaing. The sheep didn't usually make noise until they caught sight of me, so I jumped out of bed and ran to see what was wrong. Peering through the French door, I saw Charlotte pacing around by herself under the cedar trees next to the house. (All the sheep received new names that were a better reflection of their spirits. I waited for each name to emerge, from wherever inspiration lives, and Charlotte's was the first to arrive.) I was surprised to see her so close to the house and without the other two. Like all good flock animals, the ewes traveled together.

Then I saw that, though the flock was not with her, Charlotte was not alone. A tiny, impossibly white lamb tottered over to her on its spindly little legs, the remains of an umbilical cord dangling from its underbelly. The baby bleated piteously and Charlotte baaed in return. I found out later that there is much vocalization just after birth so mother and child can learn to distinguish each other's voices and locate each other quickly in the flock, in the interests of safety and survival.

Enthralled, I went out to greet the newborn lamb. Charlotte at first allowed me to get close but then started butting me to let me know that was enough. I brought her hay and water, which she welcomed with avidity. While she munched, I sat on a log under the tree to gaze at the lamb. He had blue eyes, white eyelashes, and ears that stuck straight out from his head, which was covered with a fine white fuzz. The insides of his ears were pink, as was his nose. He tripped around on his tiny mother-of-pearl hooves, bleating in a baby cry that gripped my heart.

It was drizzling, but mother and child were dry under the trees and behind the windbreak of the log pile between the cedars. Charlotte had picked the best spot on the property to have her baby. In retrospect, I think she also chose the proximity to the house for the safety and assistance I could provide. The sheep seemed to know soon after meeting me that I was someone they could trust, and, though I wasn't fully aware of it, Charlotte and I were already turning to each other like plants to the sun.

Birthday

The lamb tripped over to me, tripped away again, and stumbled around Charlotte in search of milk. I noticed then that Charlotte used a new voice to talk to her baby when he was close—a throaty equivalent of a horse's nickering. This was the intimate cooing of a mother to her infant.

The other ewe (I had named her Queenmere, Franglaise for Queen Mother, because she was head of the flock and the best of mothers) and the lamb, Chloe, arrived, drawn by the baaing and bleating. Chloe followed the little one's stumblings with excitement. Queenmere was Charlotte's grandmother but had been like a mother to Charlotte when she was little, I had been told. I had noticed that Charlotte turned to Queenmere whenever she was anxious. Now, though, after greetings all around, Queenmere and Chloe moved away to a respectful distance, perhaps at Charlotte's request.

I touched the baby on one of his trips to investigate me and he didn't seem to mind, but Charlotte decided I, too, needed to go. She came at me repeatedly with head butting, so I took that opportunity to go inside and leave an SOS message on Jane's answering machine. It was after eight a.m. by then and I figured I had waited long enough to call, given what I viewed as an emergency. I had no idea what, if anything, I was supposed to do for mother and child.

The old anxiety started fluttering in my stomach again as I worried that, this time, I really *had* taken on too much. First a horse, then a donkey, and now what was supposed to have been two sheep was four. I was learning about their care as I went along, but all of a sudden I had a lot more to learn and I had better learn it fast.

The birth of the lamb was not a complete surprise. Jane had given me a warning when she arrived with the sheep.

"This one is either very fat or pregnant," she had said of Charlotte. With six weeks gone by, I had thought we were safe from an increase in the flock.

Suddenly, Charlotte lay down and began contracting. It must be the afterbirth, I thought. She got up and walked behind a small pine tree but was still visible through the branches. She lay down again and I saw something white come out of her. She got up and began licking it. She's eating the afterbirth, I thought. But it looked too white on the ground, so I went to investigate. It was another lamb and it wasn't moving—no response to Charlotte's licking.

I didn't know whether to intervene or let mother and nature handle it. The baby still didn't move. There would be brain damage or death if it didn't get some oxygen soon. I ignored Charlotte's aggressive protectiveness and moved in to clear the lamb's mouth of the amniotic sac still covering its upper body. It didn't help and Charlotte went for me again, so I backed off, saying to myself, "Let nature run its course." It did, and the lamb never came to life.

Later I learned that a lamb will sometimes start breathing if you take hold of the back legs and swing him or her around. The consensus among people experienced with sheep, however, was that it was unlikely this lamb would have revived. The fact that there was an hour between the births of the twins indicated that something was seriously wrong, and the second lamb was probably already dead when he was born.

I was considering what I should do next when the phone rang. To my relief, it was Jane. She said there were only two things we needed to do: dip the lamb's umbilical cord in iodine to prevent infection and squirt a nutritional boost paste in his mouth. She would be over in an hour or so with the necessary supplies. I told her about the dead twin and she said it was okay to take it away from Charlotte. "Just push your way in and take it," she said.

I was unprepared for sheep care of this sort. I didn't even know how pushy I could be. But I grabbed a towel, gritted my teeth, and walked firmly up to the dead lamb. As I picked him up, Charlotte got up from where she was lying and came toward us, but I quickly wrapped the body in the towel. Not seeing that I had her baby, she stopped. I took the body to the porch for safekeeping until I had a chance to bury it. I lay the little bundle on a chair, pulled back the towel, and arranged his body in a circle, nose to tail, with his legs tugged in.

I sat gazing at the lamb. He wasn't much bigger than a cat, though of course his legs were longer. There was a little smile on his face and he looked as though he had died happy. Given the way the birth went, he may have died floating calmly in his amniotic fluid. I hoped so. Crying, I stroked the little lamb's pure white coat and talked to him, telling him how sorry I was he couldn't be with us. Then I rewrapped him in the towel and went back to my post of watching over his living twin.

The wild turkeys who had recently begun to roam the neighborhood chose this moment to pay their first visit. I heard loud gobbling from the other side of the house and snuck around to take a look. Eleven large turkeys perched on the fence, while two more, a female and a fully puffed-out male, performed a ritual dance on the ground. Were these the thirteen fairies come to bestow gifts and blessings on the newborn babe? *Not your typical fairies,* I thought with a laugh.

Jane arrived. I told her I hadn't seen the baby nurse. She said we needed to confine mother and child so Charlotte wouldn't be able to keep walking away from her lamb every time he tried to nurse and also so they would be protected from the elements. It was still the rainy season in California and, though Charlotte had chosen a good place for the birth, higher winds and heavier rains were likely. I laid wood shavings and a blanket in the lean-to attached to the barn.

Jane carried the baby in, with Charlotte following close behind, clearly anxious at her baby being removed. Jane laid the baby on the blanket. He stayed there, looking tired. While he rested, Jane showed me how to "throw" Charlotte, which meant get her down on the ground. Jane wanted to do this so she could check Charlotte's nipples to make sure they weren't clogged.

She rushed Charlotte, pinning her in one corner of the shelter, and, standing against her side, slipped one hand under her chin, raised her head up, and took hold of some wool on her rear end with the other hand. To "throw" the sheep, you start in that position, with your hip against her. Then you turn the sheep's head in to her side and pull her over onto the ground on her other side as you step back. When done correctly, it is smooth and fast, even with a large sheep like Charlotte (she weighed about 150 pounds). But to me, suddenly thrust into hands-on sheep care, it seemed rough and I was concerned for Charlotte.

I stood with one foot wedged under Charlotte's shoulder (an immobilizing technique) while Jane checked her udder. Squeezing brought no milk flowing from one of the nipples. Jane massaged the udder to pop the plug and then expressed some milk into a bottle she had brought with her. We stepped back to let Charlotte up. She struggled to her feet and moved as far away from us as the shelter would allow, which wasn't far since the space was no more than eight feet by six feet.

Jane then showed me how to tube-feed the lamb because she wanted to make sure he got some colostrum, the high-protein, immune-boosting first milk of lactation.

"Tube-feeding sounds much worse than it is," she reassured me, taking the lamb on her lap and wielding a length of rubber tubing. Charlotte stood in the corner, eyeing us warily. I was feeling pretty wary myself.

Jane put one end of the tubing in the lamb's mouth and gently worked it to the back of his throat. He seemed to swallow it easily. She then placed a syringe casing in the other end of the tubing, and slowly poured in the expressed milk. The baby did not gag during the procedure and afterward fell into a heavy sleep on the blanket, likely relieved to have a full stomach at last. Jane had me do the second feeding when she came back a few hours later, and the tube did indeed go down easily. She expressed more milk for me to keep in the refrigerator. I tried to do the milking, under Jane's guidance, but could not quickly get the knack. Not wanting to distress Charlotte more than we had to, I asked Jane to do it.

That afternoon, there I was, out there in the shelter on my own for the third feeding, holding a tiny lamb between my knees with one hand, putting the tube down his throat with the other, and somehow pouring milk into the syringe casing. I felt both scared and exhilarated—scared by the responsibility for this little life, and exhilarated by managing to do these dauntingly unfamiliar farm tasks.

The next task I had to confront was dealing with the dead twin's body. I had assumed I would be digging a hole and burying it, but Jane told me that Rae put her dead lambs (it turns out it is not uncommon in a flock for a lamb to be born dead) far out in the pasture for the vultures. I had never done this with an animal before and the thought of vultures tearing apart the body made me queasy, but then it came to me that this baby's death would not be so senseless if his body provided food for the living. So I took him out to the far pasture and placed his body, in its now stiffened circle shape, in a small clearing in the center of a grove of bushes. I lay rosemary sprigs on him (the qualities of rosemary are protection and remembrance) and placed his afterbirth next to him, which Charlotte had expelled not long after his birth but had not eaten. I told the little one again how sorry I was that he couldn't have stayed with us, said a few prayers for him, shed more tears over him, and then went back to his mother and twin, feeling bad at leaving him that way. He looked so small and alone out there.

It was fortunate that we had moved Charlotte and her child into the shelter, because the next day it poured rain. I still had not seen the lamb nurse and called Jane. She came over, concerned, and on seeing the lamb said he definitely needed food, that he had the hunched-up look you didn't want them to have. We did another tube-feeding, and then I held Charlotte's head while Jane tried to teach the baby to nurse by sticking his nose into her udder, encouraging him to latch onto a nipple. Charlotte moved from side to side. We tried it with Charlotte on the ground, too, which naturally involved another throwing. After half an hour to an hour of this (I lost track of time out there), Jane was completely frustrated. She was holding the baby by the neck with one hand and his body with the other. The baby, exhausted and needing nourishment, was like a limp rag. She turned his head to face her and I could see the frustration in her body.

"I could just throw you against the wall," she said, giving him a little shake.

"Let me have him," I said, taking him from her and cradling him in my arms, holding him for a moment against the warmth of my body. I silently sent him messages of love and encouragement. Jane's treatment of the lamb was mild compared to what happened on many farms, but it was not my way. I already loved the lamb and I didn't want his life to begin with animosity coming at him. After holding him for a few moments, I tried more gently to get him to take the nipple, but it was no good.

A veteran shepherd might have been able to get the lamb nursing, but Jane was relatively new to all this and I was completely raw. This was an illustration that good intentions and the ability to connect powerfully with animals are not enough. You have to back that up with practical knowledge and experience if you are going to take care of them properly.

Jane and I gave up. In retrospect, I should have called Rae, but I felt like I had been bothering her with a lot of sheep questions and I thought it would be too much to ask for her to come out to my place. Jane seemed experienced enough. In most things with sheep, she probably was. But this was an unusual situation, which, as I would discover, was how life was with Charlotte.

I would have to bottle-feed this lamb. I may have thought the sheep and I would just live as neighbors, but it turned out we were to be more intimate. Thrust suddenly into the flock, I found myself in the midst of an intensive course on the Way of the Sheep.

After Jane left, having given me instructions and a list of supplies I would need, I took time out before going to the feedstore to talk to the lamb and Charlotte, telling them how sorry I was for the treatment they had received, that that was not the way it was going to be, that I had a different way of doing things. I held the lamb while I talked to them. Charlotte stayed in her corner but looked at me steadily, without fear.

After that, I was with them for five feedings a day and numerous visits in between. Jane had warned me that feeding him might not be easy, that it takes some lambs a while to figure out the bottle, but this little one got it right away. He lay in my lap and latched onto the nipple with little trouble. He needed to rest frequently during the feeding and then would fall fast asleep in my arms for ten or fifteen minutes afterward.

As I watched him sleep after the first bottle-feeding, I thought how fortunate it was that Charlotte had borne twins. The year before, she had given birth to the largest lamb that Rae, Jane, and a sheep-experienced veterinarian had ever seen. When Jane came out one morning, Charlotte was near death, with the huge lamb half in and half out of her. The lamb was already dead and the summoned vet thought the labor had been going on for a long time. They managed to save Charlotte, but it took months for Jane to nurse her back to full health. The vet said that Charlotte should never give birth again, that it would likely kill her. Unfortunately, Jane was not vigilant about keeping the rams away from her and Charlotte ended up pregnant once more. The fact that she bore twins meant that they were each smaller, which made delivery easier and possibly saved her life.

Charlotte may have survived childbirth, but it appeared that it had weakened her system because her breathing became labored and she seemed to be having trouble drawing a breath when she was lying down. Jane thought it might be a return of her respiratory infection as a result of all the rain. She called the vet who had prescribed the previous course of antibiotics for Charlotte and ordered another round.

Jane had still been coming over to milk Charlotte, to try to prevent mammary problems from developing and so I could give the milk to the lamb. Charlotte resisted her interventions and Jane said she had always been "psychotic." When I asked what she meant, she said, "She gets hysterical over nothing, always acting like I'm going to kill her. She was like that from the first and it hasn't changed the whole time she's been with me. She's worse than any other sheep I've had."

I was extremely grateful for Jane's help and didn't know what I would have done without her, but I could understand why Charlotte resisted. When Jane came into the shelter, she did not acknowledge Charlotte's existence but immediately began doing whatever she was there to do, which is the way many people who work with so-called livestock behave. I always greeted Charlotte and let her know that I saw her. It is a common courtesy that we extend to humans (though many people don't extend this to children). Humans don't cooperate when they are not acknowledged. Why would we think animals would?

Once during a hoof trimming, Gabriel pulled away when the farrier tried to start on one of his right hooves, having finished trimming the left. My in-tune farrier said, "Oh, I forgot to introduce myself to this side." He stopped, talked to Gabriel from the right for a moment, and gave him a little neck scratch. After that, Gabriel stood patiently for the trimming. The farrier commented that it was a matter of respect.

In the situation with Charlotte, I wasn't about to ask Jane to do it differently. She was being so generous with her time in helping me. She could have just left me to deal with the sheep on my own, but instead took time out of her own animal care duties to come over to my place nearly every day that first week after the lamb's birth and teach me what I needed to know. Though I didn't say anything, I stepped in to spare Charlotte where I could. There was one change I could implement immediately to help her. Not liking the throwing, I bought a sheep halter. That made it easier on all of us. Jane put it on the first time, but I did it after that.

To people used to handling sheep, putting on a halter is nothing. But as it had been with Pegasus, for me it was a big deal. In fact, everything I did with the sheep was a big deal, since all of it was new and required putting my physical self forward with confidence, which I didn't have in the farm-yard. I knew about putting my body on the line. I had been doing one form or another of dance since I was seventeen, training in ballet, modern, and jazz; I had gotten my under-graduate degree in dance therapy; I had taught dance for four years. But this required a whole new kind of physical confidence. It wasn't about physical strength; I had that. It was about approaching a large animal confidently (hoofed ones have no respect for timidity), moving or handling a big animal, and accomplishing what needed to be done. This care of the sheep was far beyond what I had to do with Pegasus. While the farmyard was building my character, I walked around with a pit of anxiety in my stomach.

Jane gave Charlotte the first of the three antibiotic shots from her vet. Aware of how much time she had already given to us, I told her I would handle things from there. I sent her off with profuse thanks for helping me through the crisis.

I still could not quite believe being thrust into this hands-on life with the sheep. Now I had to figure out how I was going to give Charlotte her remaining two shots, which, again, was a big deal since I had never done anything like it before. There was no way I could hold Charlotte's 150-pound body and give her a shot (though Rae was able to do this), so I called my dear friend Mella, who had no ovine experience but had developed gestational diabetes and had had to give herself injections during her pregnancy.

Our challenge was to figure out what was bone and what was muscle beneath all that wool. We finally just went for it, and Mella did the actual needle plunging. When it worked, we were absurdly pleased with ourselves and we both congratulated Charlotte on how well she had done in this trying experience. I was weak with relief.

Charlotte's breathing problems had cleared up by the time Mella returned to administer the final shot. Charlotte was immensely patient, standing still while we again tried to figure out where to inject. Mella was as anxious as I was to cause Charlotte minimal discomfort. I think Charlotte knew that. In any case, Charlotte and I were making progress. The fact that she would stand still for us said a lot.

In those days, it seemed I was always in the shelter with mother and child. Jane had told me it would be easier for me to "yank" the lamb, meaning take him from Charlotte and keep him in the house, but I didn't want to separate him from his kind. What would that do to his socialization? Besides, I didn't mind going out in the dark and rain to feed him. It was pure pleasure to see him standing knock-kneed, ears straight out to the sides, looking up at me with an innocent wondering look in his eyes, and bleating in anticipation. He demonstrated the absolute truth of "innocent as a lamb." I loved holding him and watching him drink. While he slept on my lap after his bottle, Charlotte came to check on him, then nudged me for the horse cookies I gave her during the feedings.

The baby's name still hadn't arrived, though I called him all manner of endearments for the utter sweetness he was. I was patient, knowing the right name would come in due time. Meanwhile, he was doing well on the lamb formula, growing into the skin that had looked too big for him. In a matter of a week, he moved out of the infant stage and became a toddler.

Chloe and Queenmere continued to run free while Charlotte and baby were confined. Charlotte was upset at being separated from Queenmere, so I periodically coaxed the others into the corral connected to the lean-to. Charlotte calmed down then and was much happier. Part of her distress was, I'm sure, the cognitive dissonance created by separation of the flock—life is just not quite right when the flock is not together. In the corral, Queenmere experienced some dissonance of her own because Chloe was still small enough to fit between the railings of the fence and blithely jumped in and out, ignoring the anxiety she caused her mother. The supreme mother couldn't keep a watchful eye on her daughter when she disappeared around the side of the barn.

Queenmere the wise leader

What the Animals Taught Me

Young Chloe

There was often an animal chorus, with Charlotte calling for Queenmere, Queenmere calling for Chloe, the baby calling for milk, Pegasus (whose time on the grass had to be limited) whinnying to be let out, and Gabriel braying for Pegasus to join him.

Having Queenmere and Chloe on their own without Charlotte, who always pushed her way in and kept them from coming up to me, enabled Queenmere, Chloe, and me to bond. They were often under the pine tree next to the house, so I put water out there for them and they usually spent the night there, protected from wind and rain. Queenmere still kept her distance from me, but not as far as before. Chloe, at first tentative about being touched, was soon enjoying the caresses I gave her, pushing against me for more when I stopped.

Unfortunately, as the rich spring grass came in, Pegasus began to show signs of laminitis again, despite the sheep-shorn grass. At first, I put her in the corral, with the half door between her and mother and child. Charlotte and Pegasus communed regularly over the door, nose to nose, and I saw how circumstances were bringing all of us together. But I needed to give Pegasus access to shelter, so I would have to move Charlotte and her lamb to the old pump house out in the pasture, which would be their home for another two weeks until the lamb was big enough to be safely let out.

Charlotte and I ended up wrestling all over the pasture. Forty-five minutes later, I finally got her into the new shelter. While I sat panting and sweating on the shelter stoop, Charlotte serenely munched her hay, seeming unperturbed by our wrestling match. I was glad she didn't hold a grudge but said, "So why did you make it so hard for me?" She gave me her direct Charlotte gaze, which was answer enough.

Looking back now, I shake my head in amazement at the prolonged wrestling. If I had known then what I know now, I would have simply picked up the lamb with one hand, a bucket of grain with the other, and calmly walked to the shelter. If Charlotte hadn't come right away, I would have remained calm and let her enjoy the grass for a while, knowing she would come when she was ready. But all that calmness comes from experience. I was a rookie, so I wrestled.

Queenmere and Chloe, who had kept their distance during the journey across the pasture, now approached. Charlotte stopped munching on the hay and came to the door to call to them. There was much baaing all around as they all commented on this new development, and probably on the weirdness of their caretaker.

While they exchanged viewpoints, I looked with sadness upon the baby's formerly perfect pearl hooves, now covered with muck from tripping across the pasture after his wrestling mothers. I cleaned his feet, wanting to bring back his baby innocence, but he had taken his first steps in the world and the rest was inevitable.

First grass: Chloe and Wonder

In the new shelter, Charlotte and I became close friends. I discovered that she loved to be touched, especially having her chin rubbed. She still started to butt me occasionally, but not with much intention attached. I figured it was born of frustration with confinement and I adopted the tactic of distracting her with caresses, which worked.

One day I went out to the corral for a feeding and as usual looked over the half-door before climbing into the shelter. There stood the tiny lamb on his little knock-kneed legs, gazing up at me with tender trust, and his name suddenly arrived: Wonder. From then on, he was a constant reminder: Life is full of Wonder.

Wonderlamb

UNCONDITIONAL LOVE LESSON #2:
Letting Go of Judgment

Beginning to learn the Way of the Sheep started me thinking about how most of the animal references in our speech are negative—a bunch of sheep (mindless followers), stupid cow, stubborn as a mule, eat like a pig, dumb as an ox. Humans disparage what we want to distance ourselves from or what we don't understand. Speaking disrespectfully of a certain group reveals our negative judgments, which we may not even be aware we harbor. Animals, especially farm animals, seem to be the last bastion of human unconsciousness regarding the "other." We've learned to clean up our language regarding ethnic groups and women, but it's still open season on animals—in more ways than one!

Sheep are some of the most disparaged of the farm animals. I have had countless people ask me, hesitantly or boldly, "Sheep are stupid, right?" It seems to be a human tendency, exhibited by scientists and laypeople alike, to judge the intelligence of animals by how closely their behavior resembles ours. The further their behavior ranges from that of humans, the lower their intelligence is concluded to be. It is easier to label behavior we don't understand as stupid than to try to figure out the wisdom in the action. This is as true of the behavior of other people as it is of the behavior of other animals.

As a result of living closely with animals, I have discovered a basic truth: They have their reasons. Any behavior I have ever witnessed among the animals under my care has a reason. Sometimes the reason is obvious and sometimes I have to watch or tune in for a while before I understand.

In living closely with sheep, I have learned the beautiful logic behind the behaviors that have earned sheep such disparagement by humans. Many people dismiss the manner in which sheep run together like fish in a school when there is unexpected movement in the pasture as hysterical overreaction, but when you know that sheep have no defense against predators except escape and safety in numbers, their response makes sense. Humans ridicule a "flock mentality," but the truth is that we would probably be doing better as a species if we were as connected to each other as sheep are. The flock is actually a powerful social unit, not a bunch of mindless followers. Rather than denigrating the flock for moving as one, shouldn't we be in awe of how attuned sheep are to each other to be able to do that?

When we judge sheep as mindless followers, we don't see them for who they really are. A pure connection cannot happen with judgments blocking the way. The people who work with sheep who persist in calling them stupid are not *seeing* the sheep. Perhaps that's what they need to do in order to sell them or send them off to slaughter. Judgments enable us to keep our distance.

Sheep are as individual as other beings are. I have never met a person who did not have his or her own personality. I have never met an animal who did not have his or her own sheepality, horsality, dogality, and so on. Some people who have visited my sheep have expressed surprise that their faces are different (and they weren't referring to color). Those people really looked at the sheep, rather than allowing the common belief that all sheep look alike to distort their vision. Interesting—that's how some humans have described their enemies, as all looking alike. Somehow, if we take away others' individuality, we won't have to treat them with respect—another distancing technique that closes our hearts.

I let go of preconceived notions about sheep and let the flock teach me about who they are. The more I saw each sheep for who each truly was, the more we connected on a soul level. I could feel that level by the cord that ran between my heart and Charlotte's, or Chloe's, or Queenmere's, or Wonder's when I saw them, or even thought about them. The more we connected, the more I could see of each one. This is the deeper process of getting to know each other. When judgment is set aside, the other can shine in the fullness of who she or he is and expand even further in the sunlight of acceptance.

Wonder had a special low baa for Charlotte and a similar one for me—these were the baas reserved for his mothers. He continued to greet us with his special baa even when he was full-grown. I am deeply grateful to him and to the other sheep for embracing me in their fold and teaching me how to move as one with them. And I am proud to be a member of the mindful flock.

Having let go of judgment and opened my heart to these wooly beings, I got to experience what sheep can be like when allowed to live free in an environment of love and respect. There is still the fear and pain borne by their species all over the world and extending back many, many generations, which is in their energy fields, cellular memory, or animal archives (however you want to view the energetic storage that goes with each species, including ours) and exerts an effect on their behavior, I'm sure. But Queenmere and her flock rose above that as best they could. It has been my privilege to witness the beautiful result: peaceable kinship.

3

Gabriel the Archangel

THE ANIMALS WERE CREATING A SANCTUARY around me—a place of peace. The deepening relationships between us all expanded that peace with each day we lived together. One morning I sat on the wooden bench at the edge of the field, drinking a cup of coffee. Wonder, now two months old, nibbled wildflowers at my feet while the three other sheep, Pegasus, and Gabriel grazed nearby. Farther down the field, the turkey flock and several deer foraged in the grass. The phrase "Animal Messenger Sanctuary" suddenly appeared in my mind's eye, along with the knowledge that the animals and birds before me were messengers come to remind humans that all beings are sacred and love is the natural way of the universe.

That was the official birth of the sanctuary, though it had of course begun before that. Gabriel was the founding messenger, since he was already present when I moved to the place where it began, but it took the arrival of Pegasus and the sheep for me to catch on that what we were doing was creating a sanctuary. The vision of the Animal Messenger Sanctuary came to me fully formed that day. It was to be a safe haven where farm animals could live out their lives in peace and harmony, wildlife could seek refuge, and the message was respect for all beings.

Wonder laid his chin on my knee. As I stroked his fleecy head, I looked over at the first angelic messenger, grazing peaceably with his soul mate.

Gabriel in the lupin

When I met Gabriel, that wasn't his name. He was called only by two initials. His adopter had given him the first initials of two people living nearby in the hopes that if the donkey was named after them they wouldn't object to the braying of the new arrival. Knowing what I now know about energy, I see what this name did to him on an energetic level. It signaled that he existed on sufferance and had no identity of his own.

At a year old, Gabriel had been taken from his home in the desert after being rounded up by the Bureau of Land Management, probably by helicopter. These periodic roundups in the deserts of southern California are aimed at keeping down the population of these wild descendants of the donkeys used as pack animals by the forty-niner gold miners. The BLM then takes the donkeys around the state in trailers to sites where it holds adoption auctions.

After three years in his new home, Gabriel was still terrified of people. I was the only one he trusted, but that extended only so far—acceptance of a carrot from my hand and the occasional pat. Veterinary and other care was an ordeal for everyone involved, including Gabriel. Rounding him up was difficult and he had to be tranquilized to have his hooves trimmed. Needless to say, it was done rarely. Once, so panicked at being herded into a small corral for hoof trimming, he leapt up and threw himself against the heavy metal tubing of the fence panels. Fortunately, he didn't break a leg, but he left a huge dent in the fence, strong as the metal was. He didn't manage to escape, but the hoof trimmer said forget it, and left.

I resolved to work with Gabriel to gentle him down so care wouldn't be so hard on him. It tore at my heart to see him in terror and having to be drugged. Plus he had to wear a halter all the time and the crosspiece was wearing away the hair on his nose.

Using food, I coaxed him into one of the small corrals. When he realized there was no escape and it was only me (not some scary guy, too), he would allow me to touch him, but trembles of fear ran beneath his skin as I did. I talked soothingly to him while I gently stroked his velvety brown coat, but I knew he was living for the moment I would open the gate and let him free. When I did, he bolted as though his life depended on getting away from me.

Terrible things must have happened to him, I thought. Rounded up with a helicopter, then corralled and freeze-marked with a BLM number, which you could see on his neck. Freeze-marking is a branding technique that uses cold instead of hot to kill the cells on the skin and thus make a permanent mark. How had they managed to brand him? I presumed lassoing and then hogtying or hobbling him, which seemed likely given how reactive he was to having his legs touched.

I stopped confining him. There had to be another way to help him overcome his fear.

Two things began a change in him. First, I consulted my horse expert friends Drs. Deborah and Adele McCormick, pioneers in equine therapy and the authors of *Horse Sense and the Human Heart* and *Horses and the Mystical Path*. After visiting the donkey and his herd (this was before Pegasus arrived), they said to keep doing what I was doing with the donkey—talking to him, offering him treats, not pursuing him—but he needed a new name. His current name undermined who he was, they said.

I thought of names that would reflect the donkey's essence and support him in reconnecting with his courage. It wasn't long before the right name came to me: Gabriel. The donkey's bray was like the trumpet of the archangel and there was an angelic sweetness about him. Being named after Gabriel the archangel (the angel of the North Wind, whose name means "God is my strength") would inspire courage and strength, what he needed to overcome his fear. As soon as I called him Gabriel, I knew it was the right name for him. Every time I addressed him, I felt I was acknowledging his highest being, his powerful angelic self.

The second thing that created a change in Gabriel was the arrival of Pegasus. Not having much experience with horses, I hadn't thought about bonds between them being like bonds between people; that is, you like some people, don't care to spend time with others, and may meet only a few soul mates in your lifetime. Looking back on it, I can see that Pegasus and Gabriel were instant soul mates. They were inseparable from the moment I opened the gate between them.

Gabriel, Pegasus, and a turkey

Where Pegasus went, Gabriel went, and since she was attached to me, I interacted with him throughout the day. She modeled for him desire for and enjoyment of closeness with a human. She would trot up to say hello when she saw me or come stick her head in my door to see what I was doing if I hadn't been outside in a while.

With the arrival of Wonder, I was out with the animals many times a day. Gabriel was there for all the interactions and grew used to me being right with him, next to him, walking by him, giving him treats, and moving Pegasus and him from place to place as her grass restrictions changed. Being consistently and fully present—not just going through the motions of animal chores—was the best gentling method of all.

When Pegasus had to be confined because of the laminitis, Gabriel was most often standing or grazing near her paddock. He took forays into the pasture but would not stay away for long. If that weren't proof enough of the strength of their connection, what he did to help her healing left no doubt.

At the time, our vet followed the old-school treatment for laminitis. The treatment was based on the theory that, during an episode, blood circulation is increased in the digestive system to try to deal with the rich food (such as spring grass), which decreases blood circulation to the limbs, resulting in blood pooling in the feet, which in turn creates inflammation there. The prescribed treatment, besides allowing no grazing, is to walk the horse, even though it is painful, to get the circulation moving. Standard veterinary care now holds that walking is the worst thing you can do in a case of laminitis because it can cause the laminae (tissues in the hooves) to separate, which is exactly what you don't want to happen. Stall rest is indicated, along with anti-inflammatories and the old method of icing the feet.

This is an example of how medical treatment changes over time, a fact that underscores the importance of listening to other sources of guidance, whether from above or within. While I relied on higher guidance when it came to my own health, I didn't trust myself enough to do the same when it came to the animals. Natural medicine had been my primary medicine for years. Trusting your own instincts (or whatever you want to call inner guidance) is a basic tenet of that approach, which warns against handing responsibility for your health over to your doctor. But I was too aware of my inexperience with large animals and so did whatever the "experts" told me to do.

When I first tried to get Pegasus to walk, she refused to move. Her feet hurt too much. The companion walking we had learned from Christine wasn't going to work here because Pegasus was in pain and she wasn't allowed to have even a bite of grass, so I used a halter and lead rope. I kept telling her it would feel better once she got moving, and pushed and pulled on her until she did. It was very difficult to keep her walking for the prescribed twenty minutes and I felt terrible doing it, but the expert had told me to and I wanted at all costs to avoid the dire-sounding coffin-bone rotation in her hooves. Gabriel followed us, of course, not about to be separated from his beloved horse.

After a few difficult walking sessions, I despaired at being able to carry out this supposedly important part of the treatment. At my very next attempt, Gabriel took the lead and set off walking. Pegasus stepped off after him. To my amazement, Gabriel led us on a walk all around the property, varying the route he took, conceivably to make it more interesting. Pegasus did the whole walk with no protest. And her gait did seem to improve, an indication of less pain. Gabriel kept going until I turned toward the paddock, at which point he led us back. Every day thereafter, when I put the halter on Pegasus and brought her out for her walk, Gabriel immediately stepped out in front and led us all around the property. Each day, he continued until I let him know we could stop. I thanked him profusely for his loving help in Pegasus's recovery, for recover she did.

Though Gabriel was calm around me, he moved away immediately when I tried to do anything, such as take off his halter or brush him. After Pegasus and I had worked with Christine for a while, I asked if she would help me with Gabriel. She did a companion walking session with him in the central corral, which was large enough that he could stay away from her if he wanted but not as far as he would have been able to in the pasture. Ideally, we would have done it out in the pasture so interaction could truly be Gabriel's choice, but in the interest of time, we opted for the smaller area. I watched from the barn so Gabriel wouldn't have to keep a wary eye on both of us.

Christine's work with him was a variation on the rope work that rewards a horse in training for the desired behavior by releasing the pressure of the rope. In this case, the reward is the release of spatial pressure. So when Gabriel turned away from her, she moved in. As soon as he faced her, she took a step back. When he took a step toward her, she took another step back. Gabriel would move away again after a few steps and they would go round and round the corral, Christine walking briskly toward him until he turned to face her again.

Finally, Gabriel stopped and let her approach. She stroked his neck and talked softly to him. Then she reached up and slowly began to undo his halter. The buckle was stiff, the halter having been on for so long, but to my amazement Gabriel stood still and let her unfasten it. It was a few minutes before I understood what was actually going on. Christine held out her palm with an apple slice on it and Gabriel wouldn't take what was normally a highly desired treat, even when she held it to his lips. I saw then that he had left his body. He had resisted the captivity by moving around until he realized that it wasn't going to end and then he gave up and left his body. Standing outside the fence on the other side of the corral, I could clearly see that he was gone.

Anyone who knows animals well knows that they are incredibly present beings. They have "be here now" down cold. As with humans, it is trauma that drives them out of their bodies. Years later, I found out that, in addition to all else Gabriel had been through, he had been tied to a post for a month when he first arrived at his new home. A misguided vet had advised this as the way to get the wild donkey to accept handling. Once Gabriel realized there was no escape, he couldn't live with the terror of being tied to a post, helpless and vulnerable, unable to defend himself from any predator or human who might arrive at any moment. The only way to exist with that terror was to leave his body, the same coping mechanism the human mind resorts to in unbearable circumstances. From then on, having no escape triggered that early extreme level of fear in Gabriel and he would leave his body.

As I stood there by the barn, it broke my heart to see Gabriel go. I crossed the corral, opened the gate, and let him out. My spirits lifted at the sight of him running away, his head free at last of the halter, symbol of bondage.

After that, I used what I had learned from Christine, but modified it for Gabriel. In the open, not in the corral, I faced Gabriel and extended a hand toward him. When he looked at me, I took a step back. As with Christine, Gabriel was so amazed at the sight of a human backing away from him instead of encroaching on him that he took a few steps toward me. I backed up. He stepped forward again. After a few times of this, I walked away. I didn't need to know the details of his early trauma to know that I shouldn't press his space if I wanted to establish trust with him. That simple exchange out in the open signaled so much to him—that relating to me could be his choice, that humans weren't always there to make him do something. I did this with him every day until he walked all the way forward and touched his nose to my outstretched hand.

In retrospect, I should have had Christine work with Gabriel in the large pasture, as she would normally have done. But the universe was helping us that day. By doing it the way we did, I received a vital piece of information about Gabriel that guided me in everything I did with him thereafter and built the trust between us more surely and quickly than anything else could have.

Gabriel and his flock

From then on, I could see when he was about to leave his body and I would say, "Stay with me, Gabriel. Stay here. Everything's going to be all right. Let's stay here together." It only happened when I was pressuring him in some way, such as having to confine him for a hoof trimming and put his halter back on. I always began with a session of the backing-up technique and most often he would stay in his body when I got to the point of putting on his halter, even while he trembled with his old fear. During the hoof trimming, however, my reassurances weren't enough to induce him to stay.

With the arrival of Pegasus, the farrier came every eight weeks, which is the standard hoof-trimming schedule for horses. Donkeys can get away with less frequent trimmings, and since Gabriel's trimmings were such an ordeal, they were few and far between. When I called to make an appointment for Pegasus, the farrier I had been using didn't return my phone calls. He had always taken his time getting back to me and usually showed up late for our hoof-trimming appointments, sometimes more than an hour after he said he'd be there, and he wouldn't call to tell me he was running late. This drove me crazy because Gabriel's trimming was an ordeal for me, too. I suffered the whole thing with the trembling, fear-filled donkey and couldn't relax until it was over. So when the guy went MIA, I took the opportunity to change farriers. The one I found made all the difference for Gabriel, and for me.

Like the other people who arrived at just the right time to help the animals, Claude was a gift sent to us. He is a master farrier and showed me how the work should be done, not just in the trimming itself, but also in the handling of the animals. He had that natural ease, confidence, and matter-of-factness with horses that comes from being around them all your life. He trimmed Pegasus's hooves and then looked over at Gabriel who was standing on the other side of the fence, a little ways back, keeping an eye on his soul mate from a safe distance. "His hooves really need trimming," Claude said. "I know," I lamented, "but he's so wild, it's a problem." I told him about how the other farrier tranquilized him. He said there was no need to do that and he would trim Gabriel the next time he did Pegasus.

Two months later, on the morning of the hoof-trimming appointment, I put Gabriel's halter on. With Pegasus in the paddock with him and our backing-up sessions, this had become almost easy. I would put hers on first, and then do his. I attached a lead rope to Gabriel's halter and let him drag it around the small corral until Claude arrived.

After only fifteen minutes of Claude working with Gabriel on the lead rope, tightening up on it until Gabriel turned to face him, then immediately giving him slack to reward him for giving Claude what he wanted, Gabriel stood still, with me holding his lead slack in my hand, and let Claude trim all his hooves. Claude had to work with him a little on his back feet before proceeding with actual trimming, desensitizing the process by touching the foot then letting go, picking the foot up then putting it down, but that didn't take long either. I watched in amazement. If only Gabriel had had this treatment from the beginning, his trimmings would not have restimulated the fear from his early trauma. Better yet, if only he had had this treatment from his first contact with humans.

On the fourth foot, Gabriel laid his forehead against my chest and I wrapped my arms around his head to hide him from the world. Instead of leaving his body, he was turning to me as his safe place. And he was staying. My eyes filled with tears. We were home.

UNCONDITIONAL LOVE LESSON #3:
Letting Go of the Past/Letting Go of Fear

Gabriel came to love me enough to be willing to let go of his fear to get close to me and love me that much more. I think this is what we all do for each other. Show enough trustworthiness that the other can begin to open his or her heart, and then the love and trust spirals upward until both hearts are wide open.

Sometimes the pain and fear from the past win, and the heart stays closed. But if we are willing to face the shadows within us, we can begin to release the fear and pain that dwell there. Until we let go of the past, we will not be able to love fully and completely—unconditionally.

I had already done a lot of work on my shadows before I met Gabriel, but I hadn't let go yet. I was able to recognize when he left his body because it was something I had done my whole life. So when I was saying to him, "Stay with me," I was talking to both of us. Gabriel and I healed together. I was awed by his loving spirit—that he had managed to stay so loving, toward the other animals and toward me, despite all that he had suffered at human hands. His is the triumph of the spirit.

Gabriel climbed over tremendous fear to reach me, and in the process showed me how it is done. There is always more letting go to do—we humans are good at holding on to the past—but there is a point on the path of healing when the balance of love and fear tips to the love side. After that, love expands exponentially. The heart opens wider and ever more easily, and it is no longer fear drawing in fearful others, but love drawing in loving others. And the more love is created, the more love abounds.

Until we let go of our pain and fear, we can't see ourselves or anyone else clearly, nor can anyone else see who we really are. We may catch glimpses of each other as our beautiful spirits shine through before disappearing into the shadows again. I had glimpsed the true Gabriel in the growing atmosphere of love we were creating on the sanctuary, but when the fear-love balance tipped to the side of love, I watched with delight the emergence of his full self—strong, wise, deeply caring, and also curious and fun-loving, with a sense of humor.

One day, I saw him playing in the field with the doe who seemed to have made the sanctuary her home. They were taking turns chasing each other in what looked like a game of tag. First the donkey was "it," then the deer. When they tired of the game, they grazed companionably side by side.

When I called Pegasus and Gabriel in at night—I no longer had to round them up; they came when I called—Gabriel often ran and kicked up his heels in sheer fun. I would laugh and clap and he would do it more while Pegasus would tear toward me at a gallop. It was obvious he had been released into happiness and was feeling it more every day.

Gabriel and I had also taken to singing together. When he saw me, he usually brayed. I would answer by calling his name in the same up-and-down notes of his bray. He would keep his bray going and I would keep mine, and we would weave our song together for many measures.

Love was gathering love on the sanctuary, creating a virtual harmonic convergence of love.

One morning I looked out the window to see Charlotte leaning against Gabriel's front legs and chest, with Gabriel's head resting on her woolly back, his eyes closed. They stood that way for quite a while, basking in each other and the morning sun, a perfect picture of peace, love, and letting go.

4

The Deer Ones

AS SPRING TURNED INTO SUMMER, the doe who had been
playing tag with Gabriel in the pasture moved closer in. I
knew it was the same one because her right ear was tattered.
Sometimes in the company of other deer, she took to napping under the cedar trees next to the house, where Wonder
had been born. It was cool there and I put a bucket of water
out for her and the turkeys, who also often hung out under
the cedars, as well as on the cool cement of the patio and on
the deck railing where there was a birdbath. Not wanting
to interfere with the natural world, I did not feed the deer
or the turkeys, but they came anyway. They seemed to have
joined the sanctuary.

One morning, I saw the doe in the memorial garden,
a grove of California lilacs and a redwood that had begun
as a tribute to a deceased friend and become the burial site
for beloved animals. A stream of light from the newly risen
sun bathed her in gold and I heard her name as clearly as if
someone had spoken it: Angel.

As the foraging grew scant in the dried fields of summer, I took to leaving apples out for Angel. She didn't seem
to be leaving the property as she used to. (Deer could easily
jump the fence; I had seen them do it.) I placed the apples
under the apple tree when she was not around because I

didn't want her to associate humans with food and possibly expose herself to danger somewhere else.

One June afternoon, I stepped out on the patio and there was Angel under the nearby pear tree. Pegasus, Gabriel, and the sheep visited the tree daily as soon as the blossoms had dropped and the pears began to grow, ever hopeful of finding fruit on the ground. Angel, looking plump and healthy, moved slowly away, unalarmed but appropriately careful. The next day, I looked out the kitchen window to see her at the corner of the house in the shelter of the laurel tree and climbing rose. She looked more than plump; she looked pregnant. I wondered if that was why she had been hanging around the house so much in recent days, sticking close for safety, knowing that she was going to give birth soon and that I could be trusted.

Animals were now regularly visiting my dreams. Sometimes it was one or more of the animals on the sanctuary, but often it was another species—a bear, a sea lion, cats, dogs, rats, an owl, a hawk, sea turtles, rabbits, an opossum, dolphins, even a hippopotamus and a camel. Sometimes in the dream the animals needed my help, sometimes they carried a message, sometimes they seemed just to be stopping by for a visit—maybe checking out this new animal helper they had heard about from other animals. That night, after seeing Angel under the roses, she came into my dreams with two tiny fawns, the youngest I had ever seen. She seemed to want to show them to me. In the dream, I welcomed the babies, praised their beauty, and thanked Angel for bringing them to visit me. I awoke feeling honored that she had.

I didn't see Angel all that next day and wondered if she had given birth the night before. Had my dream been in real time?

 64 **What the Animals Taught Me**

Angel under the cedars

Two days later I was out in the field taking morning pictures of the sheep when vultures rose out of the bushes in the second pasture. With trepidation, I went to investigate, moving slowly along the path made by the animals through the brush. Then I saw what had drawn the vultures—the body of a deer lying in a thicket of bushes. Part of the hind end was eaten. Oh, sweet Angel. I tried to see the right ear to see if it was tattered, but the deer was lying on her right side.

With a heavy heart, I turned away. As I began to walk toward the first pasture, two beautiful fawns sprang out of the brush and bounded by me. They ran into the first pasture and went to the water trough. Tiny little feet, tiny black noses, tiny little beings. The youngest fawns I had ever seen—just like in the dream. Had Angel shown them to me after she died giving birth? To tell me to take care of them?

I ran into the house and called a wildlife care center to find out what I should do. They gave me the phone number of Marjorie Davis, the head of Fawn Rescue. As I made the call, I thought, how wonderful that there is an organization dedicated to rescuing fawns! Marjorie herself answered the phone and, after hearing what had happened, she said she and a helper would come right over to assess the situation. They were there by ten a.m.

The first thing Marjorie wanted to do was see the deer's body. Back at the thicket, I pointed to where the brown deer blended into the brush around her, making her hard to see. Marjorie, then eighty-three years old, ducked under branches and had almost to crawl to reach the body. She sat next to it, poked the belly with a stick, and looked for fetus bones or any sign that the deer had given birth to other babies. I had told her that I had seen Angel three days before and she had looked pregnant, but based on my description of the fawns, Marjorie said they were at least a week old and could be as much as ten days old. She held up the deer's right ear for me. I had told her, too, about the tattered ear. My heart sank again—yes, there was the tatter. So it was Angel.

Marjorie explained that the pregnant look could have been from bloating from an internal condition, perhaps a complication that set in after birth. This was a fresh carcass, she said—no maggots and the brain hadn't been eaten. She explained that vultures eat the brain early on. I was impressed by her matter-of-fact relationship with nature. At that point in my country education, I was still made a bit queasy by the thought of maggots and of brains being eaten.

Then we tried to catch the fawns. Marjorie has a setup to care for motherless fawns until they are viable and can be returned to their natural habitat. Her approach keeps the fawns wild and thus not compromised for later survival.

The fawns had gotten through the gate by the barn—I couldn't believe they had fit through the small openings in the metal grid of the gate. They were standing together by the honeysuckle on the fence, seeming at a loss as to what to do.

Moving slowly without speaking so as to avoid stressing the fawns, Marjorie, her assistant, and I managed to herd one into the first pasture, while his sister ran along the outside of the fence toward the second pasture. We heard her crying in the blackberries—she sounded like a cross between a kitten and a rabbit. It soon became clear that we were not going to be able to catch either of them. We finally got them back together in the first pasture and left it at that. Marjorie said she would give me supplies to bottle-feed them. "When they are hungry enough, they will walk right up to you and suck on your finger," she said.

Marjorie concluded that these were indeed Angel's fawns because they kept trying to head back to her body. Marjorie also felt that something had been wrong with Angel to make her stay on the property because it was not good deer habitat—not enough to eat and no oak trees; oak leaves are one of their preferred foods. Deer are not grazers, she said, adding that when deer look like they are grazing, they are actually eating the little plants amidst the grass, not the grass itself.

After Marjorie left, I tried numerous times the rest of that day to get the fawns to come for a bottle, without success. Though they wouldn't let me get too close, they looked at me unperturbed. I worried that they were getting dehydrated, until I saw them drink from the water trough. But, too young to digest leaves and other plants, they were getting no sustenance and Marjorie said they couldn't survive long. She decided they would be better off in her setup and came back to try again to catch them. Again, the fawns eluded us. Marjorie shook her head in amazement at their continued strength.

On the third try, we managed to barricade the female in the barn. Marjorie sent me in to get her. The little one was running here and there, seeking a way out, sliding on the wood floor with her tiny hooves. I took hold of her and she let out a blood-curdling scream. I imagined such a sound might shock a predator into dropping a fawn—a good defense mechanism. Marjorie had told me to put my body across the baby. I dropped into the sleeping child yoga position with her between my legs, my chest over her, but putting no weight on her. She screamed some more and I silently sent her messages: I'm your mother's friend and am here to help you; now you will get some food; don't worry, we'll bring your twin to you.

Marjorie came in with a dog carrier and I put the fawn in on the soft blanket lining the bottom. Marjorie draped the carrier with another blanket, saying that the fawn would stop kicking if she couldn't see a way out. We carried her out to Marjorie's truck and made plans to try to catch the brother the next day.

That afternoon, I went out repeatedly hoping for a glimpse of the brother to reassure myself that he was all right. He didn't show himself until dusk. When he finally

What the Animals Taught Me

appeared, he seemed unfazed by his experiences, calmly foraging (or at least, seeming to) until I tried to herd him back into the first pasture. With one bound, he disappeared into the brush.

The next morning, I asked Sparrow, my highly attuned tabby cat, to guide me to the fawn. I called upon Angel, too, to lead me to her baby. I had only gone a few steps on the path in the second pasture when I saw him ahead of me, walking along the path—behind a doe! Was it Angel? Before I could see her ear, they were gone.

I rushed back to the house to call Marjorie. "Bring the fawn back!" I told her. "The mother isn't dead."

That explained what had happened when Marjorie had tried to feed the fawn she had taken. The little one had stamped her tiny hoof in defiance and fought not to eat. Marjorie was amazed at her strength—how could this be? The baby also had her back molars, which meant that she was at least two weeks old. Fawns lie low for two weeks, wherever their mother places them, and only start following the doe after that.

So the fawns were not motherless, after all. Marjorie always cautions people not to move fawns from where they are found because their mother may just be out foraging. In our case, all the facts had seemed to point to the fawns being motherless, Marjorie assured me. She brought the fawn back and we watched happily as the little sister bounded from the carrier into the brush. That afternoon, I saw the two fawns together, nibbling in the grass. No doe in sight, but I assumed she was somewhere nearby.

I felt bad at what we had put the babies through, but how were we to know, when they kept going back to the doe's body? And I had learned so much from this event that had, after all, ended well.

But it wasn't over yet.

Three days later, I was at my writing desk when the doe and the two fawns walked by in the field below my windows. I ran for the binoculars and focused in on the doe's right ear. Angel!

So they *were* her children. The other deer must have come to die on the sanctuary—a good safe place to let go into death. Were the matching tattered ears some kind of cosmic joke? The divine trickster at work? I didn't mind being the source of entertainment, especially since the trickster had seen fit to send Angel back.

She wasn't sick. She had chosen to live here, adapting to the perhaps less-than-optimal deer habitat. She could jump over the fence when she craved oak leaves, but for the rest of the time, she could roam the eight acres in perfect safety.

Something shifted with the arrival of the fawns. After that, Angel and her children were a constant presence and they behaved like the other animals, lifting their heads in greeting or curiosity when I passed by, but then returning unperturbedly to what they had been doing: eating, or in the case of the fawns, playing.

Angel and her fawns

During the day, the fawns seemed to be everywhere; I would see them on one part of the property and then when I had crossed into another pasture, there they'd be, appearing as if by magic, like little fairies. When I called the other animals in at night, the deer were often by the dense blackberry thicket, munching on leaves. One night, the two fawns visited my dreams. We were walking together across a college campus, a fawn on either side of me. I had a hand resting on one of their backs and they were calm and self-possessed, knowing I would keep them safe. Upon waking, I saw that the sanctuary was the campus and I was the student.

One day in early August, about two months after the fawns were born, I came upon a startling sight. There in the golden field was Angel, with *four* fawns! They were happily foraging, all together. The four babies were the same size, clearly having been born around the same time.

After marveling at this turn of events in our deer odyssey, I called Marjorie to share the news. She, too, was amazed, and concluded that the dead doe must have been a mother, after all. She couldn't understand how her two babies had survived. When I asked whether Angel might have fed them, she said it was unlikely. She explained that one doe will not nurse another's fawns because she has only the amount of milk needed for the number of fawns she birthed. Cervine nursing is not a system of supply rising to meet demand.

But Angel was a remarkable deer. I was sure that she had taken care of all four fawns. Now that the deer were old enough to eat, I would help her by providing branches of grape, apple, and oak leaves for her biological and adopted offspring until they got big enough to jump the fence and forage for themselves.

Daily, I was blessed with the vision of Angel and her four spotted fawns resting peacefully in the shade of the cedar trees next to the house or of the four fawns running around the stands of bushes in the golden field, chasing each other and pronging in youthful exuberance, while Angel grazed serenely nearby.

At the end of the summer, long after the vultures and the sun had finished their work, I crawled into the brush to visit the doe who had died there. Her bones were scattered, but her perfectly intact skull lay on the ground as if it had been placed there in reverent offering. I took it back to the house and let it bleach in the sun before placing it on my animal altar.

In the years that followed, I began attending monthly sweat lodges in a nearby town held by a medicine woman of the Lakota Sioux tradition. A sweat lodge is a ceremony of prayer, akin to going to church. Raised as a Quaker and being part of a Gaia circle (Earth-based spirituality that shares much with indigenous spiritual traditions), I responded immediately to the meditation of the lodge and soon was part of the lodge community. A few years after the adventure with the deer, I was packing for a women's retreat with another Lakota Sioux medicine woman. Pondering what to take for the giveaway at the end, I realized I was ready to pass on the deer skull. I wrapped it in red cloth, as is the custom for gifts or offerings in this tradition. For a giveaway, each person brings a gift to place on the giveaway blanket on the ground or floor in the center of the ceremonial circle. The first person chooses a gift and the one who brought it then comes forward to choose one, and so on until all the gifts are given.

The person who received the deer skull told me afterward that she knew before she even walked up to the blanket which red-wrapped gift was meant for her, though she couldn't see what it was. When she drew back the red cloth, she saw why. She is a medicine woman of the Potawatomi Thunder Clan and her name, Wawashkeshikwe, means White-tailed Deer Woman. Looking at her sitting across the circle from me, cradling the skull in her lap—she had laid it reverently on the red cloth and already adorned it with sage, which is sacred—I could see her strong connection with the spirit of the deer and her treasuring of this precious gift of Deer Medicine. My heart soared at the knowledge that the doe would from then on be part of Wawashkeshikwe's sacred ceremonies.

UNCONDITIONAL LOVE LESSON #4:
Trust

I was privileged to learn the Way of the Deer. Because they trusted me, I got to see who they really are, beyond the gentle doe, the fairy fawn, and the frightened "deer in the headlights." I learned that deer are spiritual warriors. They have as much fierce determination as they do gentleness, but they know when to use each, when to stay still, and when to act. Like martial artists, one with *qi,* their energy expenditure is perfectly balanced. Deer move away from other beings only when they need to, and they know their capabilities so well that, even at the tender age of two weeks, they bound away at just the right moment, not a moment too soon or too late. They remain calm until the very moment when action is needed, at which point they leap bravely but still exert no more energy than is required.

The Way of the Deer teaches that all is not necessarily as it seems: the gentle deer is also a spiritual warrior.

Trust in a relationship provides space for us to be our fullest selves. In trust, we can step out of the headlights, out of our frozen fear, out of our fear of being revealed, and show the full range of our being. Without trust, it is difficult to be who we truly are. The people we trust the most are the people with whom we can be most fully ourselves.

There is another kind of trust, one that increases our ability to be trustworthy for others: trust in our own intuition, higher guidance, or whatever else you want to call that universal knowing. With Angel, I reached a new level of trusting the guidance that comes to me from other sources than the mind. I had already taken many steps on this path, but walking with her moved me further into the Mysteries. When I walked the land, looking around in wonder at the horse, donkey, sheep, and family of deer with whom I now shared a home, I began to trust that in our journey together I would be led where I needed to go.

As the other animals did, the fawns gave me a lesson in walking the mystical path with practical feet. I wasn't allowed to dwell only in mystical communion with them. When the fawns were full-grown, big enough to jump the fence, they rarely left, though Angel came and went. That was fine during the winter when greenery was plentiful, but in the dry summer months, they got hungry, roaming rest-lessly through the corrals looking for food, though when I had fed them, it was out in the field. This was a lesson in why it's not a good idea to feed wildlife. They had gotten used to the food I had provided when they were too young to fend for themselves. I hadn't had a choice then (letting them starve was not an option for me), but I didn't want to encourage this dependence. If the property hadn't been fenced, when I stopped supplying food, they might have simply wandered off while foraging. Instead, they stayed.

I called Marjorie to ask what I should do. She cautioned me that it's illegal to keep wild animals fenced in. "But I'm not," I protested. "They can easily jump the fence." She told me I had to make them leave, that I needed to get them outside the fence and then close the gate. Heartsore, I shut Pegasus, Gabriel, and the sheep in the first pasture, then opened the gate at the end of the drive and left it open overnight. The now-grown fawns didn't leave. Finally, I had to put apples outside the gate to get them to walk out. Feeling like I was betraying their trust, I closed the gate behind them. I hated to turn them out into the dangers of the world, but the eight acres couldn't sustain them. They stayed by the gate for two days. Perhaps they left occasionally and came back, but every time I looked, there they were. I talked to them telepathically, telling them that I didn't want to say good-bye, but we had to because there wasn't enough food for them here, how very very sad I was to be parted from them, and how I wished we could have a sanctuary large enough to provide everything they needed for as long and whenever they wanted to be there. Finally, they gave up and moved on. I felt even sadder when I looked and they were gone.

All they had to do was jump the fence to get back to the sanctuary, and maybe they did when the green returned with the winter rains, but that was the end of the family as we had known it. Angel still passed through, sometimes with other does and stags, perhaps her fawns among them, but my job now was to keep my distance and help them stay wild.

In trust, we act for the other's highest good, even when it is painful to us.

5

First Flight

I WAS WAITING FOR THE TRUCKS. They were hours later than expected and it was growing dark. The news crew that had been there since noon, even though they were told the trucks wouldn't arrive until five p.m. at the earliest, was still there and the reporter said they weren't leaving until they got the story. I was impressed by this persistence. Clearly, someone was an animal lover.

We were at a large farm animal sanctuary where I had started volunteering to learn more about caring for farm animals and birds. The trucks we were waiting for were bringing hens rescued from a commercial egg farm east of Santa Cruz. The drive was more than three hours at the speed the trucks had to go with their live load, but the time had been extended by rendezvous with humane societies and other rescue organizations all along the way to hand off some of the chickens for adoption.

It was after nine p.m. when the truck towing the stock trailer pulled in, followed soon after by a pickup. We unloaded the hens by the truck headlights trained on the temporary chicken habitat: a large enclosure with sides and roof of chicken wire to keep out the predators who roamed the hills, partially tarped to provide shade, with a wooden hen house at the upper end. Clean straw and wood shavings covered half the ground; the rest was left as open dirt for the hens to enjoy scratching and dust-bathing. Bowls of water and plentiful chicken feed awaited the new arrivals.

What was originally going to be a few hundred chickens had swelled to more than seven hundred. Staff and volunteers from other agencies had been pulling chickens out of their three-high-stacked cages in the filthy factory most of that day. Having quickly filled the many large metal crates and plastic dog carriers they had brought with them, the rescuers turned to filling cardboard boxes. In one crate, I counted thirty-six hens and, in one flat cardboard box, fifteen. When we opened the containers, the chickens did not come out. At the time, I thought it was because they had never known anything but cages, but I learned later that it was also because it was after dark, when chickens hunker down for the night.

We worked as fast as we could to get all the chickens out of the containers. We reached in and gently pulled each hen out, setting her carefully on the ground in the enclosure before reaching for the next one. I whispered over and over, "Welcome to your new life. You're safe now and it's going to be wonderful!" It was incredibly moving to see them take their first steps ever on earth. They had lived their whole lives packed in wire cages called battery cages, the bottom of the cages slanted so the eggs the hens lay roll into a hole that opens onto a conveyor belt. This is standard practice in egg agribusiness. The hens never get to see their eggs (of which they are normally protective), they never get to be outside, they don't have room to stretch their wings and can barely turn around in the space in which they are kept, and their beaks are cut off when they are chicks so they won't peck each other as adults packed into a cage.

The hens were eighteen months old. Considered past their egg-laying prime, they were going to be slaughtered, all 160,000 of them. The new owner of the farm was shutting down the operation and invited rescue organizations to take as many as they could before the rest were sent to slaughter.

The factory gave the hens no care beyond food and water. Though some commercial egg businesses might at least remove dead chickens from the cages, in this factory the rescue crew saw many dead hens and even body parts amongst the frantic living hens. The chickens in the bottom two cages were covered in feces and had lost many of their feathers; the ones on the very bottom were in particularly bad shape. The rescuers didn't take many chickens from the bottom layer of cages because they didn't think they would live. One rescuer said it was very hard to be in the position of choosing who would live and who would die. She said she had been on many animal rescues, but they usually involved taking everyone. She felt terrible as the hens in the lower cages watched them taking the hens from the upper.

The hens they brought looked bad enough. Most were extremely thin and many had lost a lot of feathers. Their combs were pale pink or almost white, puffy, and flopped over, signs of severe nutritional deficiency and lack of sunlight. Their toenails were so long—three or more inches—that the hens had trouble walking when we set them on the ground. Normally, hens wear their nails down by scratching the earth in search of insects and other delectables.

After emptying all the crates and boxes, we sat on the bales of hay in the chicken enclosure and trimmed hundreds of nails, still working by the truck's headlights. While we worked, most of the hens huddled in bunches. Some, however, woke to their freedom. They drank deeply from the bowls of water we had placed around the enclosure and then climbed in, flapping around in the water. One of the staff told me that chickens and turkeys love water; when the hose was sprayed in the bird yard, they would come running with the ducks and geese to frolic in the rivulets. In the egg factory, the hens had to peck at a red dot to get a sip of water.

Here, while some hens played in the water for the first time, others scratched in the dirt, also for the first time. Still others stretched their wings and flapped them over and over, as if they couldn't believe that they were actually getting to do this. Then some took little flying leaps, again for the first time in their lives. Several became quite enchanted with taking off from the rim of the shallow depression we had filled with water for them (it had been a wallowing trough for the pot-bellied pigs who occupied the enclosure for a time) and flapping to a landing on the other side or in the water below. I loved seeing them standing in the water. I could almost hear them saying "Ahhhh" at the wonderful sensation, on feet that had only ever stood on metal bars.

The hens

One hen jumped up on a bale next to where we sat and nestled into a sweatshirt lying there. Another came and pressed against the side of one of the nail trimmers. She stayed leaning against her for a long time, then climbed into another's lap and cuddled there for a while. It was all a revelation—for them, and for us. We were touched by the acts of trust and the reaching for comfort.

When I finally left, it was past midnight. The news crew had long gone, after getting their story at last. Some of the hens were still up when I exited the enclosure, exploring their new freedom, but most were piled into mounds, fast asleep.

I returned the next morning to continue the nail clipping. We wanted to get them all done before the next wave of hens arrived. The rescue was still under way; the number would top two thousand by the time it was over. When I arrived, the hens were basking in sunshine for the first time, and reveling in dust baths, another activity basic to life as a chicken. I was alone in the enclosure and couldn't get enough of watching the happy hens. Those lying in the dust in full sun, flapping their wings every so often to redistribute the dust over them, looked to be in utter ecstasy. Among the others, there was much clucking, squawking, running, scratching, eating, drinking, splashing, and flapping. All were clearly thrilled by their liberation and were trying out every chicken skill.

In trimming the nails, I held each little body in my lap and was moved to tears by the thinness. At first, the hen protested when I turned her over to lie on her back on my legs, but then she would nestle her head against my stomach, blink up at me, and submit to the trimming. Sometimes a hen would close her claws around my fingers, the pad of her foot pressing against my skin. I stayed still then, feeling the sweetness of this little being flowing into me. I looked into her blinking eyes and we just gazed at each other. I had never looked into a chicken's eyes, but it was the same as looking into anyone's eyes—windows to the soul.

And as with humans or any other beings, some like to commune; others have things to do and places to go. When I turned the hen back over on my lap after the trimming, some leapt off and ran away. Others didn't move and I picked up each of these to hold her to my heart, to send love and healing to her battered soul. Some stayed for a long dose; others squirmed and I put them down immediately. They had been confined long enough. From now on, *they* would get to choose how they spent their time!

To my delight, the sanctuary hired me to help take care of the chickens. The current staff had enough to do with the more than three hundred farm animals and birds already in residence there. With seven hundred more chickens, the caretaking in the hen habitat was constant. I spent whole days cleaning, feeding, and watering. It was a joy to watch the chickens become more themselves every day. They ran happily around me as I worked, sometimes pecking curiously at my boots in passing. Some of their combs began to darken and move toward the healthy upright position. Feathers began to grow back.

The hens had to master the art of perching. The instinct to attempt it was there, but when they did, they wavered back and forth on the thick branches we had moved in for them to use as perches, like people trying to regain their balance to keep from falling off a log. Perhaps they had to tone their perching muscles after their long confinement. In any case, it took quite a while for them to sit solidly on a branch.

New life

The hens also had to learn to stop piling on top of each other at night. At dusk, they began to clump and we worried that the ones on the bottom would suffocate before morning. The hen house wasn't large enough to accommodate many. After watching them cram in there to a dangerous level, we took them all out and closed off entry to the hen house, afraid there would be a mass suffocation. We placed the halves of the dog crates around the enclosure at night, open side down, to provide little houses for sleep, and then hurried from crate to crate, redistributing the chickens to prevent overcrowding. At first, they ran around, but with growing darkness, they would tend to stay where we put them, and soon the enclosure was quiet, everyone asleep.

In the sanctuary's permanent bird yard, which housed turkeys, geese, ducks, and chickens, piling up at night like this wasn't a problem. Each bird found a place in the large barn where all the birds spent the night—in the rafters, on the perches, in the cubicles along one wall, on the hay bales, or in the wood shavings. Several might share a cubicle, but ten wouldn't try to cram into it. The piling of the new arrivals seemed to be an aberration born of how they had been forced to live in the factory. It took months for this behavior to abate, though it gradually became less severe, with three-deep pile-ups becoming two, then reducing to a single level of chickens clumped close together. When we moved half of the hens from the enclosure to the permanent bird yard, they were still doing the clumping and continued it in the barn. Over time, they began to distribute themselves more around the barn and, finally, some spent the night on the perches.

Working in the permanent bird yard, I got to spend time with the turkeys who had been rescued from a turkey farm. They, too, had had their beaks cut so they couldn't peck each other. These were white turkeys with rose-hued heads that turn a darker or lighter shade depending on how they are feeling; a deeper red indicates a happy bird. They

In the bird yard

were curious and liked to interact with the gentle humans who entered the yard to care for them or who were on one of the occasional sanctuary tours. I was sitting on the ground in the bird yard one day, listening to a tour leader talk about the feathered ones, when I turned my head and found myself looking straight into the eyes of a turkey who had quietly come up next to me. On the ground, I was at eye level with him and he seemed quite taken with me, nearly climbing into my lap. I stroked his feathers and was gazing soulfully into his eyes when his head suddenly darted forward with that quick motion of chicken and turkey necks and he pecked me in the eye. Fortunately, my eyelid reacted in time and I only ended up with a sore eyeball. I could only laugh at myself. It was a reminder not to forget the practical in that mystical world of oneness: while communing, be aware that a turkey might decide to investigate something shiny.

Wild turkey at the door

Back at home, I was often treated to the sight of a large wild turkey gazing in at me through the French door. Or perhaps he was looking at his own beautiful reflection in the glass, his head glowing red—as with the domestic turkeys, a sign of happiness. The wild turkeys had taken to visiting that door or the French doors in the dining room each morning. They alternated between napping on the stoop and pecking on the glass. I didn't feed them, so the attraction was something else. Perhaps they thought the reflection was another turkey. Perhaps they were interested in seeing what I was doing inside. Or perhaps they had a message for me that thus far I had failed to receive, so one or another of them came back each day to try again.

On Thanksgiving, my guests and I were seated at the dining table enjoying a vegetarian feast when loud thuds sounded on the roof over our heads. We watched through the French doors as wild turkeys began plopping down from the roof onto the patio, one after another, like Thanksgiving paratroopers. My city friends were exclaiming in amazement at the sight when there was a racket on the deck outside the kitchen door. I jumped up, having heard that sound before.

Pegasus had climbed the six steps to the deck and was clomping around on the wood, wanting to see us. She had navigated the stairs numerous times before I had put up a rope barrier, afraid she would break a leg going back down. Today, with all the guests coming, I had unclipped the barrier. I fetched her halter and lead rope from their hook in the mudroom and opened the kitchen door. There stood the magical white horse, gracing us with the equine equivalent of beaming. I put her halter on and led her through the carpeted dining room, with pats and carrots from the guests along the way, out the French doors onto the patio where the turkey paratroopers parted before her. Again, city friends were enthralled. So was I. Though I live with these animals and birds every day, I still marvel at the gift of their presence and all they choose to bestow on me.

UNCONDITIONAL LOVE LESSON #5:
Respect for All Beings

For the series of books I wrote on natural medicine treatments of mental health disorders, I interviewed the African shaman Malidoma Somé, who brings the teachings and wisdom of the Dagara tribe to the Western world. We talked of the level of violence in the United States and he spoke of the Dagara knowledge that a society cannot be healthy if its people are cut off from their ancestors. In the West, shame and guilt have disconnected many of us from our ancestors, says Malidoma. He conducts rituals to help people restore those ancestral bonds. Turning to face the ancestors and giving them the acknowledgment and respect that is their due, regardless of the deeds of their lifetime, is the path to reconnection.

Malidoma's words stayed with me and I began to work on reconnecting with my own ancestors, which has given me a sense of wholeness I didn't have before. (So many of us who moved to California from the East Coast thought we could leave the past behind.) I also began to think more about disconnection. I realized that just as a society cannot be healthy if its people are cut off from their ancestors, a society cannot be healthy if its people are cut off from nature. The lack of acknowledgment of and respect for nature has enabled us to perpetrate planetary disaster. Humans could not continue to destroy the natural world as we have so systematically been doing if we allowed ourselves to feel our innate connection with nature, instead of frantically amassing material goods, disappearing into addictions, and otherwise checking out to keep from feeling that connection. If we felt that connection, we would not clear-cut forests. If we felt that connection, we would not pour toxic waste into rivers and lakes. If we felt that connection, we would not allow chickens to live their lives packed together into small cages so we can have a seemingly endless supply of cheap eggs.

In addition to the humanitarian issue, there is an energetic aspect to cruelty. The energy of fear and suffering being added to Earth's energy field by only one battery chicken farm has negative effects on all of us; imagine the energetic effect of the billions of chickens, turkeys, pigs, and cows enduring daily hell in agribusiness operations.

Albert Schweitzer said, "Until he extends the circle of his compassion to all living things, man will not himself find peace."

Gandhi said, "The greatness of a nation and its moral progress can be judged by the way its animals are treated."

Belgium, Austria, Sweden, the Netherlands, and Switzerland have each banned the use of battery chicken cages and the European Union has followed suit, by banning their use anywhere in Europe, effective 2012. In 2008, California became the first state in the United States to ban battery cages, mandating in the Prevention of Farm Animal Cruelty Act that, by 2015, egg-laying hens, calves raised for veal, and pregnant pigs can only be confined in ways that allow them to lie down, stand up, fully extend their limbs, and turn around freely. How amazing that even these standards—the barest minimum—have to be mandated. I am heartened, however, by this evidence of the growing recognition of our responsibility to other beings.

Respect is at the center of healing our disconnection from nature—respect for all beings, including ourselves. How much can we respect ourselves if we are willing to suppress our connection to the natural world, which, of course, includes us? How much can we respect ourselves if we are willing to ingest food infused with the energy of fear and pain? How much can we respect ourselves if we close our eyes to the suffering of humans and other beings around the world?

Respect is more than a feeling. It is recognizing the sovereignty of the other, whether that other is a chicken, a human, a river, or a tree. Sovereignty is the right of that other to exist, and to exist in the fullness of its being. So the chicken and the human must have enough room to exercise their chickenhood and humanhood; neither can live its life fully in a cage. The river must be allowed to flow freely and not be choked to death with dams and chemicals. The tree's habitat needs to be preserved to enable the tree to flourish, and, if farmed, farmed sustainably so as not to destroy the forest. There is a growing movement in the legal profession to accord sovereignty to nature; known as Wild Law, it gives a river, for example, the same rights as a human being.

The Way of the Chicken teaches us to respect where we might not think to apply respect, reminding us that it is our responsibility to honor every being. It reminds us, too, that every action we take has consequences; every action and its attendant energy adds to the energy field of the universe. We can ask ourselves before we act: Will this add to the energy of fear and pain in the world, or will it add to the energy of love and respect?

Loving unconditionally requires respect, for self and other. If we don't respect ourselves, how can we truly open our hearts? If we don't respect others, it is unlikely that we respect ourselves. Respect doesn't require that we accept all behavior, but it does mean that we treat the other as a sovereign being. I find it easier to know how to do this with humans and their (and my) complicated behavior by thinking of the soul of the person involved. When I do that, my indignation, anger, annoyance, or other negative feeling that is interfering with my ability to respect the other begins to seep away and I can find my way back to connection. On the soul level, there is always respect. Soul to soul. Descendant to ancestor. Human to chicken.

Respect has another lesson for us. As in letting go of judgment, beware of jumping to conclusions. In recognizing the sovereignty of others, we don't get to decide who they are. This is especially apropos when it comes to farm animals. My time with the chickens reminded me that we can't draw conclusions about how a species or an individual naturally behaves based on their behavior in the convoluted environments in which we keep them. Until we provide the environment that allows them to live as the sovereign beings they are meant to be, we will not have the privilege of seeing who they really are.

In loving unconditionally, the blinders that prevented us from seeing drop away and our eyes are blessed with at least a glimpse of the full glory of a chicken, human, cow, or tree. May each and every one of us be thus blessed!

6

A Sense of Belonging

THE DRIVE TO WORK WITH THE CHICKENS at the animal
sanctuary took me past a small farm. Every time I drove by,
I saw the same black-faced sheep standing in the same spot
by a barn on the far side of a junk-filled yard. From what I
could see from the road, through the high chain-link fence
surrounding the property, she appeared to be alone and
looked like she hadn't been sheared in some years—neither
of which is good for a sheep. I asked Beth, another worker
at the sanctuary, if she had noticed the sheep. Yes, she, too,
saw her every day, lamented the conditions in which the
sheep lived, and had resolved to help. The sheep stood there
in the same spot, rain or shine. From the road, we could
also see a large pen of goats, but they were far from where
the sheep stood. Beth had only occasionally seen a person
on the place.

The next time I drove by the farm, I saw a woman near
the barn. I drove on to work, got Beth, and the two of us
went back to inquire about the sheep. Through the chain-
link fence, we called to the woman. She approached warily.
We introduced ourselves and told her we had noticed her
sheep and were wondering if she might like to give the
sheep a home with other sheep. When she shook her head,
we asked if we could just see the sheep. Reluctantly, she
let us in and led the way to the barn. We were aghast at

the condition of the animals we saw along the way—goats with hooves so long they had curled up over the feet like deformed Persian slippers, dogs and cats with open sores, and then the ewe, with so much wool on her that she moved with difficulty beneath the matted, dirty, yellowish-brown mass when she retreated at sight of us.

We refrained from commenting on the condition of the animals and I asked the woman how the sheep came to be there. She told us that there used to be three sheep, this ewe's mother and sister, but they had died some time ago. She relayed matter-of-factly how the last one had laid down in the middle of the pasture and continued to lie there in the pouring rain. She said she had gone out after a day or two, rolled the ewe onto a tarp, dragged her into the open barn, and left her there, figuring she would probably die. She did. We listened to the story, appalled, but I asked only how old the remaining sheep was. Five years old. The last time she had been sheared? Never had been.

I focused on the ewe, who watched us in fear from across the small pasture behind the barn. I was determined to get her out of there. After talking with the woman about other things—the farm, her life—I came back to the subject of the sheep and she finally agreed to let us take her, not right then, but at some point. The first step, we said, was to get the sheep into a smaller area, and from there we could herd her onto the stock trailer. The woman said she would try later. I said we would be happy to help her now and asked if she had any grain to coax the sheep through the barn into the pens on the opposite side. "That door hasn't been closed in years," she said glumly, indicating the barn door. "We won't be able to shut her in." I dug along the base of the door with my boot and freed it from the dirt. Beth and I moved out of sight and the woman, holding a bowl of grain, coaxed the sheep into the pen, which had a covered area connected to it. While the sheep ate, we moved forward quickly and shut the door.

The woman wouldn't commit to a date for the stock trailer to come. We begged for her phone number and she finally gave it to us. Before we left, I gently suggested it might be a good idea to move a goat or two in with the ewe because sheep live in fear when they are alone, vulnerable as they are to predators without the protection of the flock.

We called the woman numerous times over the next three weeks. No one answered the phone. Driving by, I was relieved to see that she had acted on my suggestion. A goat that had the markings of an African gazelle was in with the ewe. When we finally managed to get through to the woman on the phone, she told us she was sick and couldn't deal with it. I waited for two weeks and then called again. No answer. We saw her outside occasionally, so we knew the animals were being fed.

A month later, Beth called me. "We have to get the sheep out of there now," she said. A neighbor had called the sanctuary to say that the farmwoman had dropped dead suddenly. Beth located a relative who gave her permission to remove all the animals. It was clear from the conversation that no one was going to try to find homes for the animals. "There are two sheep," said Beth. "We can't take them. Can you?" This had not been my plan. With Pegasus, Gabriel, and the four sheep, I felt I had enough to do. I had pictured the ewe grazing on the larger sanctuary, with all the staff and volunteers to take care of her along with the flock already there. I didn't hesitate, however. "Of course," I said, and went to prepare a guestroom in the barn for the new arrivals.

What Beth found at the farm was far worse than what we had seen on our visit. Rabbits in filthy hutches, with abscesses rotting away their heads. Equally filthy cages of pigeons, doves, and chickens. A small cage with a cat in it. In every outbuilding, Beth found animals and birds in appalling conditions of neglect. It appeared their keeper was what is known as an animal collector or hoarder. Animal collectors claim to love animals but seem not to see the terrible state in which they keep them and the resulting health problems that afflict the animals. I have heard that the next edition of the American Psychiatric Association's *Diagnostic and Statistical Manual of Mental Disorders (DSM)* will, for the first time, include animal collecting.

As the stock trailer backed up to the barn at my place, I breathed a sigh of relief. We had gotten the sheep out of there at last.

Unlike the arrival of the first flock, all was quiet in the trailer. I peeked in and saw what I had thought was an African goat looking earnestly back at me. He was actually a Barbados sheep, which has African ancestry. With his horns, gazelle-like markings, and coat of hair rather than wool, he could pass for a goat. He was small enough to fit between the wide metal bars of the paddock, so I approached him with the sheep halter and, to my surprise, he let me put it on. Isabel the ewe (her name had come to me before she even arrived) cowered at the back of the trailer.

Beth and I maneuvered her companion into the shelter, then stood outside the paddock fence and waited for the terrified ewe to exit the trailer on her own. Isabel swept down the ramp and across the paddock, her mass of wool swaying around her like a hoop skirt, running in search of her friend. Though the two sheep hadn't been together long, it was clear they were already close.

Isabel after shearing

Pegasus came over to investigate, going nose to nose with the little Barbados. Whatever passed between them satisfied her and she calmly returned to grazing. While Queenmere, Charlotte, Wonder, and Chloe hung back in the far corner of the pasture, looking nervous, Gabriel walked up to the new arrivals, sniffed them, and then let out a huge bray, a long singing welcome or perhaps explanation of where they were, as he had done for the other sheep. The new sheep looked startled at the first notes of the bray but then, like the other sheep, they appeared to listen.

I had arranged for Rae to shear that very night—I couldn't bear the thought of leaving all that wool on Isabel for even one more day. By the light from a rigged-up lamp in the shelter, Rae sheared and sheared. She had never seen so much wool on a sheep, she said. Later, we estimated that the pile of Isabel's shorn wool weighed sixty to seventy-five pounds. The annual fleece from Wonder, who was the biggest of his Columbian flock and about the same size as Isabel, usually weighed in at about thirteen pounds. We had expected Isabel's skin to be in bad condition, but Rae commented as she worked that all she found was urine scald on her rear end where the thick wool had held in the acidity, and that would heal quickly once exposed to air.

When Rae finished, she nudged Isabel to her feet. I wished Beth could have stayed to see this. There before us was a beautiful creamy white sheep, standing tall on black legs. "Probably a Suffolk mix," said Rae, as we both gazed with satisfaction at the liberation of the sheep from all that wool. Isabel moved haltingly around the shelter, as if figuring out how to move without her woolen burden. I opened the door to the pasture and she joined her sheep friend, who had been waiting just outside during the shearing. We watched as she began to move more freely, like the chickens discovering they could stretch their wings.

The next night, to my delight, I found Gabriel, Pegasus, and the two new sheep sharing the shelter, which could just accommodate the four of them. A sanctuary, indeed. Queenmere and her flock, however, continued to keep their distance.

Leopold

Leopold (his name had arrived a few days after he did) and Isabel spent most of each day in the shelter, with only occasional forays onto the grass. I began to think they suffered from the bird-let-out-of-the-cage syndrome, so used to imprisonment that they couldn't see they were free. Give them time, I told myself. After a week, however, when they had not even ventured to the other side of the pasture, I intervened. I gently herded them up to the gate between the first and second pastures so they could see it was open and that they were free to roam with the other sheep if they wanted. They turned and ran back to their shelter. Okay, so they needed more time.

After another week with no change, I facilitated interaction between the six sheep by feeding them all at the freestanding feeder under the oak tree by the barn. I had already asked Charlotte to help welcome the new ones, who, it seemed, were having trouble joining the flock. The six converged on the feeder when I filled it with hay.

Isabel and Leopold begin their new life

Leopold stood back while Isabel ate from one side of the feeder and the four crowded together to eat from the other side. Charlotte poked her head around to look at Isabel and also seemed quite curious about Leopold, who, I imagined, looked like nothing she had ever seen before. Dinner over, the flock of four wandered off and Isabel and Leopold returned to their shelter.

Clearly, it was going to take some doing to integrate the six. I hadn't realized how much of the closeness of the foursome had to do with the fact that they are family. I recalled a small sheep station I had visited in New Zealand (sixty sheep is a small operation by Kiwi standards). The owner told me that the sheep agents would comment that they had never encountered sheep like his before and ask him why they behaved so differently from other sheep. He would answer, "Because they've known each other all their lives. They're not thrown in with strangers. They have a true flock."

So did we, but now I had to figure out how the two new ones could feel part of the clan. In watching the group, it seemed to me that the original four would welcome Isabel if she seemed to want to join, and where she went, Leopold would follow. But Isabel was very fearful and retreated to the comfort zone of her isolation. Though that, too, was a fearful state, at least it was one she knew well.

I believed all this would sort itself out in time, but the process was hurried along by an unexpected event. One night six weeks after Isabel and Leopold had arrived, I went out to the barn to check on the animals after being gone all evening and found Leopold lying still in the shelter. He didn't move when I approached. Before I laid my hand on him, I knew he was dead. He had shown no signs of illness, but sheep are stalwart beings. Any sign of weakness makes

100   What the Animals Taught Me

them vulnerable to predators, so they are good at hiding it. Maybe it was cancer. Maybe it was a stroke. Maybe another casualty of old age. I sat with him and cried, told him how glad I was that he had been with us, thanked him for helping Isabel, and expressed my sorrow that he couldn't have stayed longer to enjoy this wonderful new life. Naturally, Isabel was in the shelter with us, keeping her distance, not from Leopold but from me. I talked to her, too, telling her how sorry I was that her beloved companion had died, but I promised her that she would never be alone again. I would see to that. It was after eleven by then and, after covering Leopold's body with a blanket, I went into the house. Before going to bed, I set up an altar in the living room for Leopold, lighting a candle there to keep vigil for him while I slept.

I dreamt that I went into the barn and found that I had been mistaken. Leopold wasn't dead, after all. But when I woke, the sad truth returned.

I was out in the pasture digging a grave before eight a.m., wanting to get it done before the next rainstorm rolled in. My digging seemed to make Isabel nervous and she moved near Gabriel and Pegasus on the other side of the pasture. Then she went to the gate where she could see the sheep grazing in the next field and stood there, baaing loudly. I opened the gate for her and she joined them. This seemed to be a good sign. I closed the gate after her because Pegasus couldn't be on the longer grass.

The digging was difficult. Water from the sodden ground poured into the hole as I dug and the soil was pure clay that stuck to the shovel in big clumps, making each load even heavier. But I have found digging the grave when a beloved animal dies to be deeply healing. There is something so elemental about preparing the earth to receive the precious body. So I dug on, bailing out the grave as I went and singing Gaia circle songs.

> Hoof and horn
> Hoof and horn
> All that dies shall be reborn
> Corn and grain
> Corn and grain
> All that falls shall rise again

Suddenly, a peacock alighted on the fence, shining iridescent blue even in the gray light of the cloudy day, then hopped down to join the flock of turkeys who had arrived not long before. They stayed throughout the proceedings, and the turkeys left some of their beautiful tail feathers for Leopold. Resting for a moment from the heavy work of digging, I leaned on the shovel and looked around at the dramatic world—peacock, turkeys, fast-moving clouds racing across the sky, all light and dark. And there, against the wild sky, arced a full rainbow, visible from end to end. Another offering for Leopold.

Isabel had called to me periodically throughout the burial, but I decided it was time for tough love. I knew if I reopened the gate, she would run back to her shelter and stay there. I didn't want her to go back to being alone. I wanted to help her overcome her fear and learn how to join. Already, she was grazing near the sheep—in between baaing anxiously and returning compulsively to the gate, the closest she could get to her shelter of isolation.

Though I knew it would be hard on her, I left the gate closed that night. When I came out in the morning, she was lying right by the gate and, over the days that followed, that's where she most often was. It was the equivalent of standing night and day next to the barn at her old place, the closest she could get to the familiar behavior. I knew I couldn't give in. There were bushes and trees for her to shelter under, if she wasn't ready to join the sheep in the lean-to I had made in that pasture with wood pallets and corrugated tin.

Gradually, Isabel began to explore her interesting new terrain. She had never before lived with so many possibilities. All she had known was a square pasture of grass. Now there were paths through high bushes to explore, a wide variety of leaves to nibble, a far pasture with delicious wild radish blossoms, if only she would venture that far. I was relieved when she was gone from the gate one afternoon and I saw her lying in the shade of a bush near the huge eucalyptus tree; it was the spot Charlotte often occupied. When the sheep were in the area of the gate, she could pass as a flock member, but the true situation became apparent when the others left on their frequent roamings and she stayed behind. Time for more tough love.

One morning I moved her from the gate by walking behind her, and continued in this way down to the far pasture so she could see where the other sheep were. She looked, then turned and ran back to her safe place. I did the same the next morning. This time she ventured just a little ways into the next pasture, seeming to look longingly at the other sheep before she turned and ran back. On the third morning, just over a week since I had closed her escape route back to her past, she joined the others. And that was it. From then on, she was always with them. They accepted her easily. They had not been the obstacle that kept her away.

A few nights later, I tested Isabel's flock membership by leaving the gate open between the first two pastures. When they had access, the sheep spent the night in the first pasture, near Gabriel, their natural protector. Would Isabel stay with the flock or go back to the shelter she had shared with Leopold, which was on the other side of the pasture from where the sheep liked to be?

Chloe and Isabel

Isabel stayed with the flock and showed no inclination to revisit the shelter, even briefly. The next morning she was lying near the others under the oak tree and went with them on their morning ritual of heading to the far pasture. I snuck down to see what they were doing and arrived in time to see the flock walk through the gate into that beautiful big field full of wild radish blossoms. The sheep were in single file, each close behind the one ahead, with Isabel between Chloe and Wonder. In the days that followed, I would see Isabel lying in the shade closest to Charlotte and Chloe, and when I put grain out, she chose to eat from a bowl with them. I could rest easy now, knowing that Isabel had her mother and sister back.

The Courage to Be Free

Watching Isabel return again and again to the safety of what she knew, as lonely and fearful as that life had been, made me wonder how long it would have taken her to break her pattern on her own, without my intervention. I think she would eventually have taken the steps to join the flock, probably through an intermediate joining with Pegasus and Gabriel, her natural protectors. But it might have taken a long time. As it was, I pushed her out of the emotional damage from her past into a future of belonging. If Leopold hadn't died, I would have proceeded more gently, but sometimes someone has to step in and protect us from ourselves.

As I considered what Isabel had to surmount in order to leave her gate and join the flock, I was filled with admiration for her bravery. She didn't know what awaited her, but she had the bravery to step forward and find out. What she found was a sense of belonging and, as with the chickens, I watched her blossom out from under the fear into who she really was. The fear had kept her locked inside herself. Now she opened to the flock and the joys the world has to offer.

It takes courage to open our hearts to each other and to the world. It's risky, it's vulnerable, it's scary. But that's the Way of Freedom and Belonging. The feeling of constriction in the heart, that clench in your chest that tells you the doors of your heart are closing, narrows your existence and signals that you have just stepped out of the flow of oneness that enables you to feel part of the whole, to feel that sense of belonging and connection that is the antidote to all fear.

What Isabel did went beyond the lesson of letting go of the past, of letting go of fear, which Gabriel illustrated so well (see chapter 3). The other side of letting go is taking action. What do we do after we let go of the past? We go find out who we are without the fear and other emotional baggage we carried with us from the past. It is a hugely courageous act to step into the unknown. Sometimes we are pushed, and sometimes we take that step on our own.

This morning, as I look outside, I see Isabel lying under a tree with Chloe. They are gazing contemplatively at the view, taking a break from their wide-ranging grazing. They spend their days, and their nights, side by side, and on the rare occasion that one gets distracted and wanders out of sight, the other calls to her sister until they are reunited. When I step outside, Isabel greets me in the midst of her grazing, often not even lifting her head or missing a bite, so it is a muffled baa. I laugh every time I hear it. None of the other sheep do this. It is Isabel's special signature that warms my heart because it tells me how comfortable she is that she doesn't even bother to lift her head at my passing. All is right with her world and she feels safe and happy within it. I receive the muffled greeting with joy, recognizing it as a gift of belonging.

7

The Service of Love

IN THE MIDST OF THE RAINY WINTER, Charlotte developed a serious limp. It worsened over the next few days. Her left front fetlock was swollen and she was dropped back on that foot as if the tendon could no longer hold her up. The vet pronounced hoof breakdown that was a congenital breeding weakness. The narrowness of her back hooves did not provide much of a base for her to stand on those legs either—another breeding problem. He said there was nothing to be done about the hoof, that it would continue to break down, causing leg pain until she was in pain all the time and would graze on her knees. When her quality of life became constant pain, she would need to be put down, he said. He trimmed her hoof and put a stiff bandage on her leg to give her some support and ease the pain, but he cautioned that it was only a short-term measure, not a curative.

I was in shock, but I couldn't believe this would be it for Charlotte. She had survived so much. My experience with natural medicine had taught me not to accept a doctor's prognosis. Instead, remain positive and look for a solution. In the meantime, I trimmed Wonder's hooves, too, because he had probably inherited foot weakness from his mother and was larger so his feet had to bear even more weight.

On the sanctuary, I was experiencing the fallout from Mendelian-type experiments to tailor animals to human tastes. Miniature horses tend to arthritis in their shrunken legs and dental problems as a result of their dwarfized heads. Columbian sheep were bred large to create as much body surface for wool harvest as possible. Unfortunately, not enough attention was paid to hoof quality during the breeding process and Columbians are known for their "gnarly" feet, meaning they are always having hoof problems. Their hooves have to bear the weight of those big bodies and have not been bred to support them. Most sheep breeds only need their feet trimmed once or twice a year. My Columbians did much better on a horse schedule— every eight weeks. With a whole flock, the cost of paying someone to do it was prohibitive, so, like most shepherds, I learned how to do it myself.

With the size of my sheep, this was no easy task. As with other care, I had to learn what worked best for each of them. At first, I laid them down for it, but they preferred standing. I respected their sovereignty in exchange for them tolerating the trimming. Wonder, my bottle-fed lamb, gave me the least resistance. Queenmere, in her infinite wisdom, also cooperated. Her daughter was another story, thrashing around in protesting fits until I discovered the calming secrets of leaning my head against Chloe's side, the place she most loved to be scratched, as I trimmed, along with frequent breaks for hugs.

Chloe required a creative approach to her shearing as well. Searching for a way to enlist her cooperation during this necessary procedure, I was guided to stop the shearer in the midst of her wrestling match. "I think it will work better if I lie down with her," I suggested. "Is that okay with you?" Fortunately, the shearer was willing to modify shearing form to accommodate us and I was willing to put my animals' comfort before social convention. I stretched full-length along Chloe's back. She calmed immediately and remained serene for the rest of the shearing. She was so relaxed that she didn't get up when the shearing was over, contentedly continuing to snuggle in my arms. The shearer commented that she had never seen a sheep behave like that before. She probably had never had anyone lie down with the sheep while she sheared either!

Researching Charlotte's condition, I contacted the vet at a respected sheep supply company run by experienced shepherds. He agreed with my vet and said that once the ligament goes, that's it, and there's not much you can do to prevent it happening. But Charlotte seemed better with her wrapped foot. When I took the wrapping off a week later, however, her fetlock was no better. I had ordered a stiff rubber sheep boot, usually used to hold medication against an infected hoof, which the sheep supply vet had suggested might help to support her ankle. The procedure for the boot was twelve hours on, twelve hours off. After the first round, it became clear it wasn't going to work. It held in too much moisture—not good for her already compromised hooves. Part of the problem was our rainy winters. Though we were on higher ground, the land was still squishy.

I called several animal sanctuaries that had sheep to find out if anyone had a solution. Nobody did. My intuition sent me to a horse supply store and then the drugstore in search of a Velcro wrap that could hold Charlotte's leg like a splint but without the rigidity, while leaving her hoof open to the healing air. One of the various wraps I tried worked. After that, I checked on her many times a day, putting the wrap back on when she had managed to remove it. Sometimes I had to search for quite a while to find where in the pastures she had shed it. I was becoming used to unusual animal chores.

Charlotte

Charlotte and I had a special bond—perhaps we had
been together in a past life, or maybe even more than one.
I could not bear the thought of losing her. It was hard not
to succumb to the pall cast by the gloomy prognosis, but
I knew I had to keep myself strong and positive if we were
going to find a way out of this. Instead of walking around
in anxiety, my job was to do all I could to help her and
then surrender to what would happen. In meditating on
how to do this, I got an answer: every time I found myself
worrying about Charlotte, I turned it into a prayer for her.
I called upon that technique many times in the weeks that
followed. This was the healing energy we needed.

Then Wonder started limping, favoring his right front
foot, and then grazing on his knees. I had to call upon my
prayer technique many times a day to keep from sinking
into despair. Where could I find the energy to pour into
Wonder, too, all that I was pouring into Charlotte? Could I
save both sheep from the dire fate predicted? I didn't know
how it would turn out, but I knew I felt better and received

What the Animals Taught Me

an energy boost when I focused on the love. Tuning into the love I felt for them lightened my spirits and I found the strength to take my next step, to find the next treatment. And when I was filled with love, answers arrived. In anxiety and fear, there was no space or attention for guidance to reach me and I felt exhausted.

In Wonder's case, he needed hoof medication, but the blue boot was too small for him. An image materialized in my mind: a friend's golden retriever wearing dog booties in the mountain snow. Next thing I knew I was down at the pet store, standing in the Muttluks aisle, staring at sizes ranging from Chihuahua to Saint Bernard. The store had a dog breed guide and I decided Wonder was about the size of a malamute. The booties were like bumblebees—bright yellow with black trim—and Wonder startled when he caught sight of his yellow-clad foot after he obligingly let me put on the Muttluk. Then he walked around the pasture, staring at his foot. I laughed for the first time in weeks.

As usual, to pair something good with any intervention, I gave Wonder a bowl of oats. The wild turkeys swooped out of nowhere to investigate the offering. Being the sweet-tempered sheep he is, Wonder companionably shared his treat with the turkeys. The moment of sanctuary and the hope of the malamute footwear buoyed me.

I was still asking everyone I got a lead on in the animal care world if they knew anything about Charlotte's condition or anybody who might be able to help. A vet who specializes in acupuncture for horses told me about a vet who had worked in New Zealand in a practice serving the gigantic sheep stations and, as a result, was far more versed in sheep care than most American vets are. After talking to Bill, it was clear that I had finally found someone who not only did not take the dim view that everyone else did, but actually had a method for correcting the problem. He anesthetized Charlotte so he could really work on her foot. I held her head in my lap while he did a radical trimming and shaved down the front of her hoof with a grater to help push her weight forward. He had proposed gluing a lift on the bottom of her foot to take the strain off the ligament, but after the trimming he wasn't sure she even needed it. He would come back in a few days to check. When he did, he found the foot so improved that he dismissed the need for the lift. He shaped her foot some more and trimmed Wonder, too.

One day during all of this, I noticed that the flock was no longer going to the far pasture. Thinking back, I realized they had been staying in the first of the three pastures since the onset of Charlotte's foot ailment. As Charlotte began to get better, the flock took brief forays out but returned relatively quickly. Queenmere was keeping the flock together and going no farther than the weakest member could manage. This wise and compassionate leader knew how upsetting it would be for Charlotte to have the flock leave, that she would try to follow, and this wouldn't be good for her foot. After that, I measured the degree of Charlotte's discomfort and the progress of her recovery by how far the flock roamed on a given day. When I saw them down in the far pasture again, I rejoiced. We had done it!

Later, Bill had to use the lifts for Wonder, but both sheep recovered beautifully, their hooves did not break down, and the ligament problem never returned.

Meanwhile, an even longer healing journey began with Pegasus. Every year brought a return of her laminitis, seemingly no matter what I did. The condition was wearing her down. Even after she had recovered from the painful limping, she wasn't her former light-spirited self. I realized one day that it had been a long time since I had seen her run.

The flock

I dreamt that night that Pegasus was galloping across a field, tossing her head in joy the way she used to. I was so happy—until I woke. Then the contrast between the horse in the dream and the one I saw when I went out to the corral brought an ache to my heart.

The vet diagnosed Cushing's syndrome, which leaves equines prone to laminitis and founder, induces lethargy, and compromises immunity, leading to opportunistic infections that can kill the animal. In conventional medicine, use of the word "syndrome" often signals that no one knows for sure what causes a health condition. Cushing's is said to be a dysfunction of the pituitary gland and/or the adrenal glands.

Since Pegasus received this diagnosis, I have come to my own understanding of the problem. One of the functions of the pituitary gland is to regulate growth. Since miniature horses often develop Cushing's, this indicates to me that the genetic tampering required to produce cute little horses has compromised their pituitary glands. They might be all right with that, but when another gland in the hormonal system is compromised through diet, it becomes difficult for the body to maintain hormonal balance. One of the functions of the adrenal glands, the other set of glands implicated in Cushing's, is the production of hormones that aid in the metabolism of carbohydrates. The hay available for horses has been genetically modified to have a higher carbohydrate content for the purpose of rapid fattening of livestock. The hay is too rich to be used as a long-term diet. The result is much like the epidemic of diabetes among humans as a result of the high-carb American diet: an epidemic of Cushing's among horses and donkeys. Like diabetes, equine Cushing's, founder, and laminitis all stem from a problem in metabolizing sugars.

As if one dire diagnosis weren't enough, on the same visit that the vet informed me Pegasus had Cushing's, he said the coffin bones in her front feet had rotated, the end result of her chronic condition. I could have X-rays done to confirm this, he said, but he was sure they had. I had thought rotated coffin bones were a death sentence, producing permanent painful hobbling that destroyed quality of life thereafter. But the vet recommended a farrier who knew how to trim hooves for the rotated bones and actually help the feet. Trimming in the standard way would cause Pegasus more pain, the vet cautioned. My expert farrier had left California, so I was relieved to hear of Mike. I scheduled an appointment for the next week.

The following morning, in the twilight state between sleep and waking, it came to me to get liquid arnica (arnica oil) and pour some in the grooves in the soles of Pegasus's feet to bring down the inflammation. By applying it that way, the arnica could be absorbed up into the foot, to the site where it was needed. I bought the oil that day and it seemed to help. I used it only for a week because I didn't want the oil to soften her already tender hooves.

Pegasus

On his first visit, Mike explained matter-of-factly that he could trim Pegasus's hooves according to the new position of the coffin bone and, with regular trimming, all should be normal again in about a year. I was elated at this news. After just that first trimming, Pegasus began roaming farther afield, a sure sign that the pain level was down.

During the trimming, Mike and I talked about horse maladies and treatments. He mentioned a bodyworker who specialized in treating lameness in horses. She had sold a couple of vets and him on her technique when they took before and after videos and saw the improvement. He wasn't suggesting this for Pegasus because she had an underlying condition, plus her musculoskeletal system needed time to adjust to the reshaping of her hooves. Body-work might be helpful later, but she wouldn't be able to hold it now. Nevertheless, an inner voice told me to get the bodyworker's name and number from Mike.

I called Cindy to come work on Charlotte. I figured my precious ewe could do with some structural realignment after all that limping. Though the bodywork brought a new ease to Charlotte's step, the greatest gift from Cindy was the herbal formula she gave me for Pegasus. She knew of a miniature horse with Cushing's who had lived to be thirty-five on this formula, which contains milk thistle, burdock, licorice, and kelp. New research on laminitis indicates that it may be a disease of toxicity; toxic buildup may also be an issue in Cushing's. Milk thistle supports the liver, which processes the toxins in the body. Burdock is a blood purifier, so also aids in detoxification. Licorice enhances adrenal function, the glands implicated in Cushing's and vital to carbohydrate metabolism. Kelp is high in minerals and also supports metabolism. A winning formula for this condition.

I did not want to put Pegasus on pergolide, the veterinary drug of choice for Cushing's. Originally a human drug often used for Parkinson's, it had been banned from the human market due to valvular dysfunction effects. The drug targets the brain neurotransmitter dopamine. Animals don't like their brains messed with. Vets assured me that horses don't notice the pergolide because it's at such a low dose, but I don't believe it. How does anyone know what the horses are noticing? In my experience, animals are sensitive to every shift, internal or external. Pergolide has saved many horses' lives, but I was looking for another way.

The herbal formula, unlike the conventional drug, would address the underlying problems. I started Pegasus on it and the results were dramatic. The very next day she stopped both the excessive sweating she had been exhibiting and her prolonged licking of the mineral block, presumably signs of her Cushing's. Over the next week on the formula, her energy lifted as well.

Yet another gift for Pegasus came from the owner of a horse-boarding facility who also takes in rescues. As a result of the high-carb hay problem, horses arrive at Michelle's facility with founder issues, in sufficient numbers to prompt her to develop a protocol for caring for them. Like me, she turns to holistic solutions wherever possible. She had found that low-carb hay was key to preventing laminitis and founder. (The very fact that this hay is available indicates increasing recognition of the problem.) Michelle also told me about low-carb pellets that can be used to deliver herbal supplements; you need to mix the dry herbs into something and the standard feed is high-carb. She further mentioned hearing that some people had had good results using the herb vitex for horses with Cushing's, though she hadn't tried it herself.

I knew of *Vitex agnus-castus,* also known as chaste-berry, for its application in restoring hormonal balance in women. I googled horse Cushing's vitex—and there was the next gift. A horsewoman told of how a daily dose of vitex had brought down the Cushing's titers (blood levels) in her horse. Other anecdotal evidence lent similar support. When I looked up the medicinal qualities of the herb, I found that it supported the pituitary gland and dopamine—like pergolide, but without the side effects. If that weren't enough to persuade me to try it, *agnus* is Latin for "sheep." I took that as a sign, and the highest endorsement of the herb!

For three years now, Pegasus has been on low-carb orchard grass, Cindy's herbal formula, vitex (three weeks on, one week off), and low-carb pellets to deliver the herbs.

She has had no recurrence of the laminitis, and her feet are back to normal under the expert farrier care. My happy horse again runs up the hill with me at dinnertime, tossing her head and taking off in a gallop in response to my clapping. Dream come true!

One morning after Pegasus had recovered, I sat on the stoop of the shelter while she ate, talking to her and looking at the beautiful view of the Sonoma range. Swallows swooped in and out of the barn, used to our presence. They were building a nest that included long strands of white hair from Pegasus's mane. I'd also seen crows gathering bits of wool left on a tree trunk by the sheep giving themselves a tree massage. As I rubbed Pegasus's withers (on the back where the mane begins), she nibbled my neck and the back of my head, nuzzling in my hair. The first time she did this with me, I knew I was in, having watched Gabriel and her give each other these love nibbles. I thought of the adage that what you love to do as a child is your heart work for life. It is certainly true for me—there was nothing I loved more as a child than animals and writing.

Charlotte joined us, pushing in for hugs. She, too, gave me her special caress, flicking her soft fleecy ear against my cheek in ear kisses, like the eyelash butterfly kisses we give children. All was well on the sanctuary.

Until a few months later, when Charlotte's udder began to swell.

Mastitis, said the vet, unblocking the teat, injecting it with antibiotics, and taking a culture. The culture came back positive for staph. The vet told me that the soil throughout our county is infested with antibiotic-resistant staph due to rampant use of antibiotics in the livestock industry. More fallout from human practices at Charlotte's expense.

The udder, which shrank after the antibiotic injection, started swelling again. Another unblocking and more antibiotics worked for a while, but on the third visit, the vet could not get the teat unblocked. The only solution was surgery to remove the udder. Charlotte was an elder sheep and I didn't think she would survive the operation. Even if she could, I thought the stress of going to the hospital and being separated from her flock would be too much for her.

Between the vet's visits, with his prediction that the antibiotics probably wouldn't work for long, I used various natural remedies to try to knock out the staph. When something helped, her udder would begin to shrink, raising my hopes, but then it would swell back up again. In addition to hot compresses and lots of vitamin C, I tried grapefruit seed extract, colloidal silver, mushroom extract, immune-boosting tincture, echinacea and Epsom salt soaks, homeopathic remedies for mastitis, and oregano and thyme essential oil rubbed on the udder. The last made her sick, even though I diluted the oils. The rest helped, especially the mushroom extract, which strengthens immunity. The udder shrank to the size of a grapefruit and then went back up almost as big as a basketball. Charlotte's radius of movement diminished as the large udder made walking a struggle, but she remained enthusiastic about me and about food.

Then one morning Charlotte didn't eat any hay and even refused her mash. To give her body a rest and keep her warm and dry, I laid down straw in the barn and confined her to quarters. She seemed relieved. When I was giving her a mash with her latest remedy in it or just sitting in the straw communing with her, Sparrow, the telepathic tabby, was most often there, rubbing against Charlotte and me or meditating, head up, eyes closed, paws tucked in, focused inward. I was sure she was helping with the healing. She had always been that kind of cat, accompanying me on the morning and evening chores and acting on anything I asked her to help with, such as dealing with the rat who had taken up residence in the barn and was chewing through plastic storage containers and creating a smelly mess. When I asked if she could do something about the rat, she sat in the hay for two days—again, meditating—and, after that, the rat was gone. I saw no evidence that she had killed it; she usually showed me her catches. I think she simply communicated to the rat that we needed him to move on.

Over the next several days, I offered Charlotte all the foods she adored—pears, apples, oats, soaked barley. She ate nothing. I began to think the staph had gone systemic. On Sunday, she was withdrawn and in such clear discomfort that I didn't disturb her with treatments. I had done all I could and it was up to Charlotte to decide whether to stay or go.

The rest of that day and into the night, I kept offering her food, just in case, but to no avail. Mostly I just sat with her, talking to her, telling her what an amazing sheep she is. It was past ten when I stood in the barn doorway after kissing her goodnight, looking back at her one last time and hoping she would still be with us in the morning. My hand was reaching to turn off the barn light when, suddenly, there came to me an image of Charlotte standing by the blackberry thicket down the slope from the barn. I had seen her there the day before I had put her in the stall and wondered fleetingly what she was doing down there when she could barely walk.

"Blackberry leaves!" I said aloud. I grabbed the clippers and a bowl and went to cut leaves by the dim light cast from the barn doorway. When I presented the leaves to Charlotte, she gobbled them up, finishing the small pile and looking up at me expectantly. "Oh, you remarkable sheep!" I exclaimed through happy tears, and rushed to cut more. I cut and cut and cut and she ate and ate and ate. I tried grain again, but she would have none of it. I went back to cutting and she greeted the sixth bowl with the same enthusiasm as the first. She liked it best when I fed the leaves to her by hand. She looked steadily at me while she chewed. I thanked her for showing me what to do. Sparrow wove between us, picking up on my elation and, I think, pleased with the results of our healing work.

When I finally went back to the house that night, I looked up blackberry leaf online and was amazed to find that its primary medicinal property is "drying and shrinking." It also helps cleanse the blood and is full of vitamin C. Just what Charlotte needed to shrink her swollen udder and combat the staph infection.

All the next day I cut blackberry leaves for Charlotte, thanking the blackberry bush as I did. I also tried apple leaves and grape leaves, both of which she ate but not as eagerly. I sat in front of her and held the blackberry leaves out to her. She consumed them quickly and met my hand for the next one. We gazed at each other in appreciation and I felt her contentment. Everything was going to be all right.

That night, her udder already looked smaller. Before I went off to bed, Charlotte began licking the exposed cement around the base of her stall, and continued licking. "Mineral salts" came into my head. I poured sheep salts into a bowl for her and she licked and licked at the rust-colored mound, replenishing her depleted trace minerals. From then on, I made sure she had the salts near her and she continued over the next days to lick them frequently.

The following morning, I got the message to get watermelon for Charlotte. It was as simple as that: "Get watermelon." It was not watermelon season, but I went in search of them and came back with two organic melons of the round variety. I cut one into pieces and Charlotte ate the entire melon, rind and all. I knew that watermelon is good for the kidneys, but when I looked it up, I found that it is also high in vitamin C and helps decrease joint inflammation. Charlotte knew what to do for her legs, which were sore from the odd gait she had to adopt due to the udder and probably arthritis.

The day after the watermelon, Charlotte ate the combination of organic oat, kamut, and barley flakes I gave her. I bought them in bulk at the health food store because the local feedstores didn't carry organic grains. A horsewoman I knew had told me she had healed a horse's melanoma by switching to organic grains. This is basic to natural medicine and common sense: the body needs healthy food as its building blocks, and especially so when there is illness.

The next morning, Charlotte wanted out of the stall. She joined the other sheep at their mound of breakfast hay, eating with her former appreciation, and hobbled at a fair clip along with them when they left on their grazing rounds. I was amazed at this rapid recovery. Charlotte had used up another of her nine lives and come back for more.

UNCONDITIONAL LOVE LESSON #7:
Listening

Charlotte and Pegasus, through their brushes with death, taught me the Way of Healing. If I had stayed at the level of anxiety and fear I felt at the beginning of their illnesses, I would have become crippled in my ability to tend them. The anxiety and fear would have both exhausted me and kept me from receiving the information I needed to help them heal. As it was, the Way of Healing actually increased my energy, so I was able to be a better and better caretaker. Paradoxically, the more I stayed in my heart, the less fear I felt. I thought that if I allowed myself to feel fully my love for Charlotte and Pegasus while they were so ill, my heart would break at the prospect of losing them and my fear and grief would immobilize me. In fact, the more I opened my heart, the better I felt. In that upward spiral of love, I received energy, messages, faith, hope, and trust—all of which opened my heart more, to receive more, to give more, to receive more, upward into healing.

Instead of feeling depleted by all the trips to the barn, the seemingly endless search for and administering of solutions, and the roller coaster of emotions with the alternating improvement and worsening in the illnesses, I found a steady path of love and joy in the moment. I soaked up the presence of Charlotte and Pegasus while caring for them. It was the illness version of the Buddhist chop wood, carry water mindfulness. I learned that mindfulness need not be a discipline practiced; it can arise spontaneously from the fountain of love in the heart. Approached from the heart, each task was a service of love; each task became easy when

I did it from my heart. And each time I returned from the barn, I was larger in spirit.

The Way of Healing is the service of love that heals both the cared for and the caretaker. Serving from the heart is the antidote to the fear, anxiety, worry, and grief raised by the illness of a loved one. Serving from the heart prevents burnout.

The Way of Healing is also the path of listening: to higher guidance, to intuition, to ancestors, to nature, to dreams.

One day amidst all these troubles on the sanctuary, I sank into doubt. Maybe I wasn't supposed to have a sanctuary. Maybe all this was a sign that it was too much. Maybe I was supposed to be doing something else. That night a wild turkey visited me in my dreams. Someone had smashed his toes with a hammer. He held his foot out to show me, gazing trustingly up at me. He had complete faith that I would help him. And of course, he was right, for my heart went out to the little one holding his foot out for me to see.

When I woke, I thanked the turkey and went back to the barn. My path was clear.

All the guidance we need is there for us. We have only to tune in, ask the question, and listen.

Horses know what to eat in the wild to treat a health problem. We have that same knowing, if we just return to it. Herbalists of yore got messages from the plants. We can, too, if we honor that quiet space inside us and open to receiving.

After my healing apprenticeship with Pegasus and Charlotte, I was a much better listener, open to all sources that came in light. I began to receive guidance on even small daily details and in unexpected places. I was in a supermarket buying a bottle of wine when I passed a bin of cantaloupes. I don't normally buy food in chain stores, but the cantaloupes were on sale, so I stopped and touched one, about to pick it up. I got the clear message, "Don't buy me. I was raised in slavery." I felt the plants forced to grow in earth depleted of nutrients and soaked in pesticides. A wave of compassion washed over me and I patted the cantaloupe, thanking it and sending it love, telling the whole bin how sorry I was they had been grown that way, and moved on.

Society today trains us to dismiss the voices of talking cantaloupes if we are fortunate enough to hear them, but the herbalists of yore regularly received communications from the plant world and were widely respected before people were taught to fear them. Mainstream science, even as bound as it is to the material world, has measured the electromagnetic fields of humans, other animals, and plants. Each is surrounded by its own field. The new science, as so eloquently explained by quantum physicist Amit Goswami, PhD, has demonstrated other realms of experience besides the limited one based only on our five physical senses, and is exploring what energy fields contain and how they function. The concept of morphic resonance, made famous by biologist Rupert Sheldrake, PhD, author of *Dogs That Know When Their Owners Are Coming Home and Other Unexplained Powers of Animals,* explains how energy fields connect us and how information is transmitted through them.

Whether it was through the energy field or some other means that the cantaloupes communicated with me, my experiences with energy fields since then have confirmed for me that there is a wealth of information that we can access there. The guidance I received during Charlotte's and Pegasus's illnesses led me on a new path of healing. I learned some energy medicine techniques and I now have a practice in energy healing for animals. As part of my work,

I am constantly refining my listening, my ability to receive, in whatever form the information comes to me.

Listening requires connecting—with another's energy field, with a higher power, with that quiet place within. To connect in this way requires an open heart. Plants do not speak to those with closed hearts. Nor do animals. Or if they do, we don't hear them.

Serious or protracted illnesses can test our ability to sustain an open heart. Before my initiation into the Way of Healing, I had attended family and friends in serious injuries and illnesses. I did so with caring and helpfulness, and was good at staying present, but the emotional and physical strain of it all wore me out. In the intensity and exhaustion of the experience, I sometimes felt tense and irritated, signs to me of a closed heart. And when I was no longer needed, I would collapse.

Not long after my experiences with Charlotte and Pegasus, my mother became seriously ill and I flew across the country to take care of her. In two weeks of caring for her around the clock, I didn't experience a single moment of tension, irritation, or silent protest, even through the sleep deprivation of her ringing her bell many times during the night to call me for help. When the ringing broke through my sleep, my first impulse was love. My heart leapt to the sound of the bell and I jumped out of bed to go to my mother's aid. During her daytime naps, I cooked and cleaned. I finally understood how mindfulness translates into daily life. Before, I thought this was a discipline I had to practice to master. Now, I discovered that it comes naturally when you have opened your heart. I did the work in gladness, honored to be able to help and happy for this time with my mother. My only concern was trying to ease the physical pain she was experiencing. It was truly the service of love. And the purity of the energy nurtured me as much as her. At the end of the two weeks, far from being exhausted, I flew home feeling refreshed. With the help of Pegasus and Charlotte, I had learned how to walk in love.

8

Eternal Connection

Our beloved archangel flew home. Being a stoic desert donkey, Gabriel managed to hide how ill he was until the week before his death. During that week, I didn't know he was leaving. I approached each day with the hope that this would be the day that the medicines began to work to restore Gabriel to his full self. Other illnesses had taught me that the pattern of recovery is not a continually progressing upward line, but more like a lightning-bolt pattern, with setbacks and gains alternating in a slow rise toward health. Keeping this pattern in mind made it easier to be positive in the face of setbacks.

Gabriel stopped eating hay or mash or anything else I offered him, but, like Charlotte, he turned to blackberry leaves. With the sores in his mouth that were part of his condition, I thought the tiny thorns on the leaves would hurt. But, also like Charlotte, he knew what he needed. When I again looked up blackberry leaves, I discovered that, among their other medicinal properties, they help to heal sores in the mouth. Wise archangel.

Part of his treatment required mouth rinses to help heal the sores. I could not do this without tying him up. So there we were, standing by a pole, another human about to tie him up again. Before I did anything, I told him what we needed to do and apologized for having to tie him, knowing he had spent that horrendous month long ago tied to a pole and terrified. I explained that I would do the rinse as quickly as I could and untie him as soon as we were finished. Finally, I told him that the more he helped me, the faster it would be over.

Gabriel fought throughout the procedure. Instead of leaving his body as he had done for years whenever he had to be confined, he was fully present—and angry. As hard as this made it for me to do the rinses, I was thrilled. It may have gone against all horse-training principles, but I didn't care. He hadn't left his body. He had gotten angry. This signaled to me that he had finally healed from his past and that he trusted me enough to be himself with me instead of behaving as he had been taught to do out of fear. It was up to me to figure out how to give him the care he needed without tying him up. I couldn't solve it then, but it was something to work on when he was feeling better.

A few days later, on a Thursday, the vet came again. There was nothing more he could do for Gabriel. He suggested that we give him the weekend to see if he started eating again. If he did, he might recover, said the vet. If he didn't . . . I was crying, and the vet told me how his elderly father had stopped eating, how the family had tried to get him to eat, and how he (the vet) had felt that it was his father's choice, that people should get to decide when they are ready to go. He suggested that maybe that was what Gabriel was doing.

I was relieved not to have to make the decision about euthanasia. I had grown up with the view that this is what you do to relieve an animal's suffering. But then I met Gail Pope, the director of BrightHaven, a "healing arts center for animals," which is home to senior, disabled, and special needs animals—cats, dogs, and farm animals and birds. An education center as well, BrightHaven teaches about holistic care, particularly hospice care and transition. BrightHaven rarely resorts to euthanasia and the result is profound. When an animal is nearing death, a vigil by staff and volunteers (as well as the other animal residents) begins so the dying one is never alone. Homeopathy helps ease discomfort, and the resulting death is most often beautiful and inspiring. Passage to the other side becomes a voyage of grace, in which all participate.

Gail and BrightHaven changed my view of euthanasia. When it came time, I would do my best to help my cats through their passage without it, but I wasn't sure I would be able to do the same for the large animals. When a horse, donkey, or sheep went down and could not get up, I didn't know how long I could stand to let them endure that. I prayed that if Gabriel needed to go that it would happen quickly for him and that we could do it on our own, without veterinary intervention. It would be so hard on him to spend his last moments on Earth afraid because a stranger was nearby. I didn't want him to have to go through that.

On Friday, I was back and forth to the paddock, trying to get Gabriel to eat. As with Charlotte, I tempted him with every treat I could think of, but he ate nothing. By nightfall, I knew he would be leaving soon. I sat on the barn stoop and cried. Sparrow came and nestled in my lap, staying while I cried and told Gabriel how much I loved him, how glad I was that he was here, that I would miss him, and how I wished I could stroke his ears one last time. He hadn't wanted me near him and moved off when I got too close. Not wanting to stress him, I left space between us. He did not lie down, as if he knew that he wouldn't have the strength to get up again.

After getting something to eat, I went back to the paddock. By then it was nine o'clock. Before I saw him, I could hear his labored breathing. He was standing in the middle of the paddock and did not move away when I approached. I held a small bowl of water to his lips so he could moisten them. He dipped his nose and seemed to welcome the water, so I offered it to him periodically over the next hour. I sat down by his head and he stayed next to me. I told him again how honored and happy I was to know him, that I wished he could stay but I understood if it was time for him to go. Then I asked him to forgive me for all the mistakes I had made with him. I listed them, asking his forgiveness for each, from the time I kept him in the small corral in an attempt to overcome his fear to the time I let a hoof trimmer try to desensitize him with a rope on his leg. "Please forgive me for all the ways I didn't understand what you needed," I said to the beloved donkey.

Gabriel turned his head to me then and lowered it close to mine. He let me stroke his forehead and his ears and neck. I cried more at this gift of forgiveness. I continued stroking his velvety head and said softly, "Gabriel, let's take your halter off." He was still wearing it in case I needed to give him something. I couldn't bear the thought of him dying with his halter on. He kept his head near mine and let me take off the halter.

I promised Gabriel then that I would rescue two donkeys in his name—two because, as close as he had been to Pegasus, he had been yanked from his clan in the desert and hadn't gotten to live with another donkey for the rest of his life. In Gabriel's name, these donkeys would get to live together and with Pegasus, and I would do with them all that Gabriel had taught me.

I left him to put the halter out of sight in the barn; I wanted him to be in complete freedom when he died, without even a glimpse of the equipment of restraint. When I returned to my place next to him, Charlotte came over and stood at my other side. Gabriel still didn't move away. I sobbed into Charlotte's woolly neck. She stayed and just let me hold her. When I touched Gabriel again, he moved away. He went to be near Pegasus, who was grazing in the night. I felt he had said good-bye to me and wanted just to be with Pegasus now. When I left, they were close together.

Gabriel

The next morning, I at first thought I saw him standing by the water trough, but then I saw him lying down by the blackberries, the wildest place in the paddock. He was dead. He looked beautiful and felt so soft to my touch. He was lying peacefully as if he had finally lain down right before he went. The archangel would know when it was time. Perhaps that had been his spirit I saw up by the water trough, close to the other animals, free from all pain, and drinking celestial water.

I wanted to bury Gabriel where he had chosen to die, by the blackberries. A strong neighbor helped me dig the large grave and we buried my precious donkey—a heartbreaking but healing process. During the burial, the other animals were off grazing. When my neighbor had gone, I spread apple pieces in the grass by the grave and all the animals came. When they had finished eating, Wonder walked up the mound of the grave, planted his front feet squarely at the top, sniffed the daffodils and narcissus I had placed in a jar as a flower offering, and then simply stood there for a long time. Communicating with Gabriel, I think. I had often seen them nose to nose in the pasture, as if having long conversations. Charlotte crossed the edge of the mound to be with me. The other sheep sniffed around a bit, then went to lie in the shade by the barn. While Wonder stood atop the grave, Pegasus slowly walked the whole area, smelling the ground. After I had hugged Charlotte and thanked her for all her help the night before, she too left, along with Wonder.

I focused on Pegasus then, for Gabriel had been her dear partner. She looked sideways at me every so often as she circled the grave. She stopped at the spot where his head had lain. She began to nose and lick the ground there. I could see traces of blood, probably from his mouth sores. She licked and licked to get all the blood out of the dirt. (Remember, horses eat only plants.) Then she smelled around again, stopped at another small area, and started licking the ground there, nosing away bits of stone and tiny sticks to clear it. She did this in four areas, and in each I could see traces of red she had uncovered. She took a long time, licking the areas down to bare dirt, taking in every bit of Gabriel's essence, the last she would have. I sat on the grave and wept, watching her perform this tender and lengthy ritual. When she was finished, she took a bite of blackberry leaf from the nearby thicket and then slowly moved off.

I asked Gabriel to visit me in my dreams and he came almost immediately—and has been coming ever since. In one dream, not long after he died, two donkeys joined Pegasus, followed by a third, who climbed into my lap, curled up, and went to sleep.

The animals grieved for Gabriel. The sheep and Pegasus stayed close together, seeking comfort in each other. They stopped roaming, hardly grazed, and could most often be found in the barn, even in beautiful sunny weather. It looked like the universal process of grieving to me—closing down one's world, turning inward to mourn the departed. We all mourned and then, gradually, mourning gave way to life.

Two years later, tragedy struck again and we mourned anew. Charlotte was twelve years old, which for large sheep is elderly. One day, I made her a bed in the stall, to get her out of the rain and give her a break from struggling after the flock. I wasn't consciously aware that she would never come out of the stall again, but perhaps on some level I knew because I put Wonder in with her that night. He emerged the next day in grief. He stopped eating and would only nibble at the grass occasionally. When he did, he didn't appear to be eating much, if any, but rather just going through the motions of a lifetime. Mostly, he simply stood, looking off into the distance. He knew before I did.

Charlotte went downhill fast after that. There was nothing really wrong with her. Her body just couldn't go on. It became harder and harder for her to get herself to standing and then to lie down again. I understood that she was beyond remedies, so I focused on giving her all the healthful foods she would eat (including blackberry and grape leaves), and on our remaining time together. Charlotte had always looked at me with a sharp, alert, connected look. Her eyes sought mine, seeking connection, and she continued this even as she neared her end. We sat in the stall, gazing at each other, and the perfect, pure connection that was ours flowed between us. It was a joy to serve her in every way. The joy grew as my heart opened more each moment, even as I knew I was losing her. This was far more than the Way of Healing. This was the service of love into the beyond.

The other sheep didn't normally look at me like Charlotte did, but Wonder started seeking my eyes after the night he spent in the shelter with his mother, as if he could see her in me, resting there in my heart.

Charlotte, who had taught me so much, had one more lesson for me.

Five days after the stall vigil began, I found Charlotte lying flat when I went out to the barn at six a.m. She tried to rise when she heard my voice, but she couldn't stand or even sit up. I propped her against me and fed her blackberry leaves. She ate one bowl and left the second, the first time she had ever done that. She fell into an exhausted sleep, her head in my lap. When she woke, she struggled to get up, then subsided into exhaustion, only to struggle again.

Here is the lesson. We were in perfect harmony and could have done this on our own, but I became afraid that she was suffering too much. I called the vet. I let my worry for Charlotte interfere with our ending of grace. I took her dying away from her.

We had two and a half hours before the vet would arrive. Charlotte had come to me in my dreams the night before. In the dream, I was lying with her, my body along hers, my arm around her, as she was dying. So that's what I did in waking life. (Only later did I realize that she was showing me in the dream how to attend her in death.) At first, my lying there with her seemed to calm her and we lay in loving silence. Then she began to struggle and I moved away, thinking she needed no touch on her body, the better to be able to leave it.

I leaned down at one point to kiss her and her ear did not respond to the touch of my cheek—no fluttering ear kiss on my cheek. She did not appear to see me either. Then I saw that she was coming and going—the process of death. When I leaned down later, her ear fluttered in response—the last ear kiss I would receive from her.

Charlotte

As the process continued, with me praying to the Goddess to take Charlotte quickly, I saw that we could do this by ourselves, but I didn't want to leave her to go cancel the vet appointment and I still feared that she could go on for days like this, as the vet had told me can happen. Fortunately, the vet was an hour late. If Charlotte and I had had yet another hour after that, I think she would have been gone. As it was, the intervention was jarring and broke our process.

Sparrow, who had, as usual, been there to help with the healing, sat on my lap next to Charlotte as our beloved sheep left. I tried to keep my focus on Charlotte even while I thanked and said good-bye to the vet.

I deeply regretted cutting Charlotte's dying process short. It would have been so like our love to go through that ending together, fully, all the way. I was with Charlotte's rhythm, connected to her process, riding it with her in its ebbs and flows. I knew now, after going as far as I did with her, that the suffering ebbs and flows as the spirit leaves the body in increments, pulling free by fits and starts. Sharing the dying, like sharing the living, is precious. Charlotte had shown me that I could trust myself to do this with an animal in my care.

With humans, we often get to experience the grace as well as the grief of death, because cutting the process short is not usually an option. Euthanasia for animals has clouded our thinking about their departure. In some cases, euthanasia may be a blessing, but to use it in every case deprives all involved of the completion of the natural cycle of life.

That morning, before Charlotte died, I had opened the door of her stall and put a small panel of fencing across the doorway so Pegasus and the sheep could see her one last time and say good-bye if they wanted. I fed them breakfast in that area. Wonder came over and stood by the door, not eating, looking at Charlotte lying asleep, her head in my lap. Pegasus joined him. Later, after Charlotte was dead, I removed the fence panel and was sitting on the threshold, Sparrow in my lap, when Pegasus came back. She nudged Charlotte's nose and gave a nicker, the sound reserved for her loved ones. Wonder did not return.

We buried Charlotte by moonlight that night. My dear brother and sister-in-law came to help, though it was a two-hour drive for them after a long day of work. Before we lowered Charlotte into the grave, I sank my hand into the wool on her side, through the gap in her blanket shroud, holding onto her wool for the last time. Then Sparrow did an amazing thing. When I sat back on my heels, she climbed onto Charlotte's body, went to the same place where my hand had been, and kneaded her paws in the wool there for a long time. A last gift to Charlotte. We did not proceed with the burial until Sparrow was finished and had climbed down from this last blessing.

I had cleaned out Charlotte's stall and opened it to the other animals. Wonder and Pegasus spent the night of Charlotte's burial in the stall together. The next day, Wonder continued his standing vigil for his mother. My heart broke again when I saw him with his forehead resting against the trunk of a tree—the picture of utter grief. I had never seen any of the sheep do that. He stood that way often over the days that followed.

Two days after Charlotte died, Wonder ate a little hay again and I felt the first lift of my spirits. It was short-lived. He resumed his fast and would take nothing I offered. He was alert, obviously not sick. Whenever I checked on him in the barn area, which was many times a day, he looked directly at me with a clear, steady gaze. Not asking for anything, just looking at me with his full being. I silently asked him if there was anything I could do to help and the answer was a gentle no. I asked him several times over the next few days if I should call the vet. The answer was a firm no. I had learned my lesson with Charlotte, so I honored his process, whatever it might be.

It became clear to me that he was taking himself out. He was nine years old and perfectly healthy, but he couldn't bear to live without his mother. Nine days after she died, he completed his journey.

I had not seen Wonder in the barn stall since the night of Charlotte's death. I had also not seen him lie down. He seemed to be weakening, though, so I was sticking close to him. I thought today might be his day because his gaze was no longer alert. He seemed to be already partly gone. Pegasus was in the stall where Charlotte had died. Wonder slowly made his way there, and I followed. He took his place next to Pegasus, turned his face to the corner, and then lay down, at last. Seeing that he was going, I cradled his head in my lap. He moved his head back and forth a few times, and then he left.

I held him and sobbed, burying my face in his wool, breathing in his precious familiar smell. Pegasus nudged him twice and I stroked her warmth, glad for the comfort of her presence. I communed with him for a long time, deeply grateful for being there at the end, even as I reeled from the shock of his death so soon after Charlotte's.

Pegasus stayed with Wonder all morning, despite the fact that I had covered him with a sheet. She did not move from his side to see what the sheep were baaing about when Mella and her husband, Scott, arrived to help with the burial. She did not move when Scott, whom she doesn't know well, appeared at the door. She did not extend her nose to greet Mella. We needed her to move so we could lift Wonder's body and carry it out to the grave, but she did not move when I placed a bucket of hay for her at the other end of the stall to coax her away. She did not move when I pulled off the sheet that covered Wonder, nor when I asked her to move, explaining why we needed her to. At last, I pushed on her gently and she shifted, but only a few steps. She was not going to leave Wonder. I finally got the message of how important this was to her and stopped trying to get her to move. How beautiful was her loyalty to Wonder! We ended up working around her.

Sparrow was nowhere to be seen, though she had kept me company in the shade of a nearby laurel tree while I dug Wonder's grave. We buried him next to his mother, with a headstone that matched hers: Beloved Charlotte, Beloved Wonder.

Charlotte and Wonder

The day before Wonder died, a mockingbird began her spring singing. She fell silent in the early morning hours on the day of his death, remained silent for the whole day, and only resumed her song with the following dawn.

What Wonder he brought, what Wonder he wrought.

UNCONDITIONAL LOVE LESSON #8:

It's Not About You

With the deaths of Charlotte and Wonder occurring so close in time, I felt the veil between the worlds to be very thin. My beloved sheep were just on the other side of the veil and I could almost touch them. The rawness of death had stripped away the illusion of vast separation between the worlds, and I saw then how close they actually are. I felt the presence of the other world. It was just along my skin. If I could somehow dissolve the gossamer layer that separated us, I would feel the brush of my beloved sheep's wool.

I asked Wonder what it was like for him now and he sent me a dream. In the dream, I was the one dying, along with other people. We slipped from one world (life) to the next (death) and back again. "I am going," I told someone who was bothering me with everyday details. I wanted to be left alone because I was so near. I could feel how close I was to dying, to slipping from one world to the next. I wasn't sad to be going. It was like taking a journey, a trip I wanted to embark on. I desired to be left alone so I could devote my whole attention to the task of making it through that thin veil into the other world. It didn't require physical effort. It needed attention and focus, like praying.

When I woke, I felt that Wonder had been telling me about his last days.

What an honor it was to be part of the passage, to offer what comfort I could to my beloveds passing over. Participating in the full cycle with an open heart that is not about the grief one feels but about the love eases the pain of grief.

Burying the beloved, staying fully present and connected, eases the pain. Celebrating the one who died, with memories, fully honoring who they are, eases the pain. Gabriel, Charlotte, and Wonder taught me the beauty and grace of death—the Way of Dying.

When you truly walk the Way of Dying, you know that it's not about you. It's not about *your* grief, *your* loss, *your* tragedy. It's all about the one passing over. That being is completing the cycle of life and it is an honor, a blessing, and a privilege to bear witness. As with the Way of Healing (see chapter 7), you are there to serve in love. When you are able to stay in your heart, you feel joy as well as grief. Joy for the love in your heart, joy for the very existence of the being you love. Joy for the gift of this being's life, even as you cry at its ending.

When Gabriel and later Charlotte were so ill, it was easy to feel dread in approaching the barn each morning. How would they be this morning? Would they still be here? My heart broke even at the thought of the beloved animal departing. Gabriel taught me well, so when it came to Charlotte, I would gather myself together before I walked out my door. That way I would be able to meet Charlotte with a fresh heart—love not fear, acceptance not dread, belief not defeat, her not me.

With Wonder, his choice was different, so rather than focus my belief on healing, I focused on respecting his decision. With Charlotte, I knew she would love to stay. That wasn't wishful thinking on my part. She had a strong will to live—she really was like a cat with nine lives—but her body was giving out on her. My job was to summon all the healing I could to help her stay, and then let go of the outcome. In Wonder's case, his body was fine, but his soul chose to go. My job was to offer him food and drink and the option of changing his mind but, ultimately, to support his choice.

The message of my experience with the passing of Gabriel, Charlotte, and Wonder was that sanctuary is not only the freedom to live in peace, but also the freedom to die in peace. To provide this peaceful passing, I had to call upon guidance frequently and listen with an open heart, as I had learned to do in the Way of Healing. Calling for guidance allowed me to step aside. With dying, as with life, when the self lets go into oneness, the whole process just goes better.

Paradoxically, even forgiving ourselves for what we perceive as our missteps in supporting the dying one involves letting go of it being about us. Lamenting what I might have done wrong separates me from Charlotte or Gabriel or Wonder (in life and beyond) because it closes my heart in fear and anxiety over having made a mistake. With those regretful thoughts, I am back to it being about me. Considering what worked and didn't work, what would be good to do and what to avoid in future situations is constructive. Regret is not. Drawing conclusions for future application is about others. Regret is about me, and serves neither me nor others.

Not forgiving ourselves closes our hearts in the same way as not forgiving others. It may help us let go and forgive if we realize that not forgiving ourselves pulls the energy back from connection with the beloveds. Not forgiving also closes the doors to guidance and visitation.

A pair of cats visited me in my dreams last night. Simone and Bentley were a part-Siamese brother and sister pair who moved in with me when they were about eleven years old and lived with me until they died. In the dream, we were in a new house together and they were happy. As in life, Bentley was just content to be with me. Simone, who in life loved water, was playing delightedly by a small pond with a stream of fresh water flowing into it.

For the nine years since Simone died, I have felt a stab of guilt whenever I think of her because I did not know at the time what I needed to know to save her from her illness. What she taught me later saved Sparrow, but that was not enough for me to forgive myself. Only since realizing how not forgiving myself, how making it about me, closes my heart to Simone and cuts off our connection have I worked on forgiving myself. To do that, I focused on my love for her, reconnecting the golden cord that joins our hearts. My guilt disappeared as I made it about us, rather than about me.

Recently, I asked Simone and Bentley to join the animal council that helps me in my healing work. They took their places by my side, with the other cats on the council. The dream came after that, telling me how happy Simone is to have the flow (symbolized by the fresh water flowing) reestablished between us.

Just as our ancestors await our acknowledgment if we have yet to turn to them and offer it, our animal beloveds on the other side are waiting for us to get over ourselves if we haven't already so the stream of love between our hearts can flow again.

9

A Promise Fulfilled

EIGHTEEN MONTHS AFTER GABRIEL'S PASSING, I fulfilled
my promise to him and rescued two donkeys in his name—
or, rather, he did. It began with a notice on the bulletin
board at the feedstore. All it said was "Free donkeys," with
a phone number. Feeling Gabriel's breath on my neck, I
called.

Bud had seven donkeys running wild in the open fields
behind a lane of houses. His house was in foreclosure and
the bank wanted the donkeys out of there. I asked about
the donkeys' history. He was a bit vague, but I gathered that
he had originally placed at least two donkeys in the field
and at some point there was a female and an ungelded male
and the herd multiplied. Over the years he had occasionally
put up notices at the feedstore to thin out the group. One
donkey had drowned when the fields flooded. They received
no care, aside from a rare flake of alfalfa. As for hoof trimming, he said the gravel in front of the water trough helped
chip their hooves down.

The donkeys were nowhere to be seen, so I went in
search of them. I walked through the fields, which were
littered with loose lengths and rolls of barbed wire, rust-
ing scrap metal, and other hazardous junk that could cause
roving animals serious injury. In the farthest field, I came
across the herd. At sight of me, they grouped behind the

one who was clearly their leader. They were all a tawny sand color, except for a ghostly white one, who turned out to be a neighbor's donkey. Aside from him, I counted five adults (two of which were male), one foal, and one adolescent.

The leader gazed at me with a strong, clear look. He was equal to any threat. I noticed, though, that he had bloody scrapes and gashes on his neck. In fact, he looked battered. I learned later that everyone in the neighborhood had been hearing the donkeys' fierce fighting. The younger male was challenging the leader. So far the elder was still in charge. This is what happens in the wild, but this wasn't the wild. There was no room for a donkey to give way and move on to new territory. If the humans were going to keep all these donkeys in one area, in my view, they had a responsibility not to allow the donkeys to hurt each other, or to keep breeding.

But that was what I was there for. Catching the donkeys was going to be a problem, though. Bud had no smaller area in which to corral them. In response to his previous feed-store postings, he said, people had just backed a stock trailer up to the gate, put hay or grain in the trailer, and donkeys had gone in.

I called the director of a horse rescue organization and she arranged a stock trailer to help me get two of the donkeys out of there. The sanctuary and I had moved to a new location by that point and the fenced area on the new property was not large enough for me to offer a home to more than two. I felt bad about breaking up the group and didn't know how to choose who would get to live out their lives on a sanctuary and who wouldn't. I was hoping for the elder male so I could tend to his neck and also because he would probably be the hardest to place. Everyone would want the darling foal. Without a way to corral the donkeys, the decision would be out of my hands anyway. I asked Gabriel to decide. After all, this was in his name. I figured he could talk with the donkeys and they could come to a decision together. Meanwhile, I prayed for good homes for all of them.

With the stock trailer backed up to the fence, we put hay near its entrance and inside and moved out of sight. The donkeys had come for the flake of alfalfa Bud had put out earlier to bring them in from the far fields, but none of the donkeys went into the trailer. Perhaps if it had been high summer when there was little to eat, they might have risked it to get the hay and grain, but they weren't desperate. After an hour, we all concluded that it wasn't going to happen. We would have to try again another day.

Weeks went by. Then Bud called me one morning to say that he had two of the donkeys in a stock trailer and did I want them.

"Who do you have?" I asked. Not that it mattered.

"It looks like we got two males," he said.

So the old donkey and the young one who had been fighting with him, I thought. That was good. I would have them both gelded and the fighting would stop. Bud explained that a man from a sustainable farm had left his trailer for donkeys to wander into, but he only wanted females. Two donkeys had entered the trailer when Bud happened to be out there and he had closed the door behind them. Gabriel had chosen. I told Bud to bring them on over.

The farmer backed his trailer up to the paddock gate at my place and we let them out. It was October 28, three days before Halloween and the Day of the Dead, when the veil is thinnest between the worlds. As soon as the donkeys emerged from the trailer, I could see that the old leader was not one of them. Gabriel had chosen the young male and one of the females.

Gabriel's promise: Sylphide and Raphael

The donkeys had never been in a trailer, but the good
news about being neglected was that they didn't suspect
humans of nefarious deeds. They rushed out of the trailer,
scared, as anyone would be by such a large change, but not
terrified. They investigated their new environment with
cautious interest. Their eyes opened wide at sight of Pegasus
and the sheep in the next corral, and even wider when the
herd of cows on the ranch next door galloped down the hill
to stop at the fence dividing the properties and stare at the
newcomers. One of the neighbors at the donkeys' former
home had a horse, but I thought it likely the donkeys had
never seen a sheep or a cow. There seems to be an affinity
between donkeys and cows. Just as the cows next to the

sanctuary's previous home had communed with Gabriel, these cows took to visiting more after the donkeys arrived than they had when it was just Pegasus and the sheep.

Pegasus was greatly interested in the new arrivals, neighing and tossing her head on her side of the fence. (I kept them separated for a while for safety's sake.) Neither she nor the donkeys approached each other, though. When watching from a distance established whatever needed to be established, it was Pegasus who made the first move. She stepped up to the fence nearest the male donkey for a nose-to-nose greeting. The sheep would keep their distance for weeks.

It was unexpected to be with donkeys whose primary feeling toward me was curiosity—so different from Gabriel. Then again, I knew so much more now, thanks to him and all I had learned from the many sources of guidance. I had talked to these donkeys from the beginning, back at their former home, telling the herd what was coming, why I couldn't take everybody but that I was praying for good homes for all of them, and that two of them would come live on the sanctuary with Pegasus, the sheep, and me. Then after the two arrived, I told them I was sorry to have separated them from their family, but it wasn't safe or healthy for them to stay in that place. I welcomed them to the sanctuary and told them how happy we were that they had joined us. I asked Gabriel to help them make the adjustment to their new life.

The male donkey let me scratch his head and stroke his ears that very afternoon, and soon after, the female did too. She had a dancer-like way of moving and I named her Sylphide—our donkey sylph. I asked Gabriel what the male donkey's name should be. The answer came: Raphael. For some reason, I resisted. Twice, I asked, "Are you sure?"

He was. Now I wonder what I could have been thinking. It's the name of another archangel and it suits this donkey perfectly.

The donkeys brayed throughout the first night. I felt their anxiety as I listened in uneasy sleep. The next day Sylphide paced most of the day. This was the first time they had been enclosed, but the area wasn't that small, with grass, blackberry bushes, an oak tree, a shelter, clean water, and plenty of hay. I didn't think the enclosure was creating her anxiety. I had the sinking feeling that the adolescent donkey was her child. If the foal had been hers, it would have come into the trailer with her. Nevertheless, equines get upset at being separated from their children. This is so obvious as to be ridiculous even to bother saying. But as with human slaves, those who treat horses and donkeys as property consistently deny the instinct that exists throughout nature—a mother's deep love for her children. And children for their mother, as Wonder so heartbreakingly demonstrated.

I told Sylphide I would go back and check on her family. Bud didn't return my phone call, so I drove by the next week. If the donkeys were still there, I wanted to try to figure out if one of the young ones was Sylphide's or belonged to another of the females. I didn't see any of the donkeys and Bud wasn't home.

After two days of braying, Sylphide and Raphael calmed. I proceeded slowly with them because they had no negative imprints on humans and I wanted to keep it that way. I would need to be able to put halters on them in the interest of future medical care and hoof trimming, but I followed my instincts in an experiment of love. Would love be sufficient to bring them to halter? I believed it would. This was different from what I had done with Pegasus. She

was used to people when she came to me, had probably been "trained," and was accustomed to wearing a halter. The donkeys were wild. My approach was to caress and talk to them constantly—to show up in their lives every day.

Showing up is the task of the spiritual warrior, says Angeles Arrien, anthropologist and educator in the Four-Fold Way of indigenous wisdom. By "showing up," she means being fully present. This consistent presence is the foundation of any relationship and, as I had learned with Gabriel, the best gentling method with animals. To me, being fully present means approaching another being from my heart. This had worked for me with feral cats and it worked now with Sylphide and Raphael. Soon they were enjoying being brushed.

The barn at the new place had three stalls, all connected and each with its own door to the outside. I left all the doors open. When I came out to give dinner to everyone, Sylphide was often in the narrow center stall. She would stay where she was as I pulled hay down from the loft above her and would eat unperturbedly as I had to squeeze by her repeatedly to prepare and distribute mash to everyone. Then she began to stay in that small space while I brushed her.

I had put a rope halter on the ground next to the donkeys' feeder so they could get acquainted with this foreign object and bestow their smell on it. One day while brushing Sylphide, I showed her the halter and then simply put it on her. She was completely fine with the whole procedure. Love was more than sufficient! Raphael resisted at first. I didn't force it, explained why we needed to do this, and eventually, he, too, accepted the strange procedure.

To my surprise, Pegasus warmed up slowly to the donkeys. Because of the way that she and Gabriel had become almost immediate best friends, I had assumed her relationships with Sylphide and Raphael would be similar. We had moved out of our mourning period and I thought she would be thrilled to have donkeys around again. That was not the case and I realized how special her relationship with Gabriel had been. Raphael clearly adored Pegasus, but she was taking her time. The sheep did not fully trust Raphael until he had been gelded.

I had been waiting to schedule the gelding until Raphael was used to the halter so his first veterinary experience would be less traumatic. Now that he accepted the halter easily, I had my nurse friend Molly give him a tetanus shot and then set the surgery for the required three weeks later. The week before the surgery, I started Raphael on homeopathic arnica, which helps keep down swelling and bruising from surgery, and I continued it for the week after. I also explained to Raphael what was going to happen and told him I was sorry we had to do this, but it was a necessity in our overpopulated world. People and animals had a responsibility to limit their procreation.

I also asked Gabriel to help us through Raphael's gelding. It's preferable not to geld during fly season, but fly season was upon us and I could wait no longer. The day of the surgery, fog rolled in (sending the flies back to bed) and stayed for days afterward, until Raphael's incision had a chance to close. I'm convinced Gabriel was responsible for the beneficial change in weather.

With all this preparation, Raphael recovered beautifully. His days of ignorance about the potential nefariousness of humans were over, however. He did not let me touch him for weeks.

Once the donkeys were acclimated to their new home and Raphael safely gelded, I could let them out onto the larger property during the day. With the sheep now comfortable with their donkey companions, the whole group often grazed together. During apple season, we began our day with an excursion to one of the apple trees for me to pick breakfast fruit for everyone. With the sun just coming up and in the balmy cool of a summer morning, the animals followed me in a line along the slope of the field in front of my house to the apple tree. We were in heaven on earth.

As the months passed and Sylphide did not change in size, I sighed in relief and, if truth be known, a bit of regret that she had not gotten pregnant before the gelding. I knew it was better that she hadn't because of the inbreeding issue, but I was sure that Gabriel, separated as he had been from his family, would have liked his legacy to be a holy trinity.

The donkeys didn't bray much anymore, but one night Raphael's calling seeped through my sleep. I half woke and listened, wondering if the braying was prompted by the coyotes we had been hearing yipping and barking of late. They sounded close and I was grateful for the protection the very presence of the donkeys provided the sheep. A mountain lion had taken out several sheep across the valley. The neighbor there said the deer that daily visited her land were nowhere to be seen the week before the attack on her sheep. I knew by the deer near my house that the mountain lion hadn't ventured into donkey territory. I wasn't worried and went back to sleep.

The next morning, I couldn't find Sylphide. She didn't come when I called. The fenced animal area had several sections and groves of trees. After looking through all of them, the only place left to look was the ravine below the eucalyptus trees. Oh no, I thought, the braying had been Raphael telling me that Sylphide had fallen or become trapped somehow. I made my way down the steep slope along the fence line with the cattle ranch and, sure enough, there was Sylphide at the bottom. She was standing in the brambles, facing the fence. She must be caught on something, I thought. Then I saw a small animal on the other side of the fence, facing her. It was a calf. But where was the mother? That was just like Sylphide to watch over someone else's off-spring in need, I thought, as I clambered down.

As I got closer, I saw it was no calf. The distinct large ears told me all—this was a donkey. Sylphide stood patiently by the fence. I'm sure she knew I was going to take care of this odd situation. I spoke softly to her while I tried to absorb what had happened. A rivulet of water ran along the bottom of the ravine, passed under the fence, and continued down the ravine on the neighbor's land. The bottom rail of the split-rail fence between the two properties had fallen. I could only guess that Sylphide had given birth right at that gap, and when the baby had stood up, he was on the other side. The baby was still wet and there wasn't enough water to have soaked him all over like that, so I presumed the birth had happened not long before. Raphael had been calling because Sylphide had separated herself from him to find a protected place to give birth.

Talking to mother and child all the while, I climbed over the fence to the utterly precious little donkey. He looked at me, slightly unfocused, still dazed from birth, I thought, but unafraid. I couldn't believe how long his legs were. How had Sylphide stayed the same size for so long with all this inside her? I scooped him up and he lay limp in my arms, perfectly fine with me holding him. I climbed awkwardly back over the split rails and placed the baby on the only patch of bare ground, by the little stream. Sylphide nuzzled him immediately and he almost fell over.

Concerned that he wouldn't be able to navigate down here in all the brambles and underbrush, I thought I had better take him up the hill to the open grass. Lulled by Sylphide's patience while I had been getting her baby back over the fence, I picked him up again. Sylphide shoved me against the fence—once, twice. I immediately set her baby back down on the ground. Before I could retreat up the hill, she turned on me and gave me one-two-three with her back hooves. I had seen her do this to Raphael when she wanted him to back off. The kicks are so fast you don't see them coming. She had me pinned against the fence and could have killed me if she had wanted to, but she held back. If she hadn't, she would, at the very least, have broken my leg. As it was, her kicks got me from my shin all the way to the top of my thigh and hurt like hell. "Okay, okay," I said, backing painfully up the hill. "I'm going." She knew what was best for her baby and I had been an idiot to do anything more than restore him to her. She trusted me enough to know I was helping her when I did that. But once they were reunited, she wasn't taking any chances. After all, I had separated her and Raphael from the rest of their donkey tribe. Who knew what I would do with her baby?

As I dialed the vet to find out if any special care was required, I thought back to that first baby, our precious Wonder, and my anxious SOS to Jane after his birth. How far I had come! Not only did I know so much more about taking care of all the hoofed ones, but I trusted that what I didn't know would come to me when I needed it. I had lots of help, from earthly and unearthly sources.

I wasn't perturbed by the kicks, despite the pain. They meant nothing in my relationship with Sylphide, only a heads-up not to interfere with mother and child. She had her reasons, so I had my bruises.

I had come into life on Earth with a strong connection to animals that had been undeterred by potential or actual injury. Even being bitten in the face by a Saint Bernard when I was two years old, which required a hospital visit for stitches, did not affect that connection. I had no fear of dogs before or after that event. When I was four, I would climb into a pigpen, a large jungly pasture of gnarled trees and high grasses, and head down the paths worn through the undergrowth in search of the huge pigs who lived there. I persisted in doing this, despite my mother's taboo. Under the training of the Animal Messengers on the sanctuary, I had removed the doubts that creep in during adulthood to obscure the knowing we are born with. I had returned to that innate trust in oneness—kicks or no kicks. Plus I knew a whole lot of practical stuff now, too!

Supporting Sylphide in her wisely safe choice of the ravine, I took hay and water down to her, placing it at a respectful distance from her and her baby, who stumbled through the brush after her whenever she moved away. The vet had said the only thing I had to do was make sure the baby was nursing. When I had first watched the pair, Sylphide had kicked out when he tried to nurse. She wasn't aiming for him; it was just a flick of the foot that I would later see her do when she needed to focus on something else, such as a stranger approaching, the message to her child being that this is not the time for nursing. I realized later that she had pushed him away at first because she was trying to determine if I was going to try to take him again. When I assured her that I wasn't and brought her food and water so she could stay where she was, she saw that there was no threat. Then she relaxed her vigilance and let him nurse.

I wondered how long it would take her to leave the ravine. It would, of course, be on her timetable. To my

 158 What the Animals Taught Me

amazement, she brought her foal up to the barn at dinner-time that very same day. I couldn't believe that the baby, whose gait was still wobbly, had been able to navigate the steep hill with all the thick tree roots and rocks in the path.

Sylphide and Ulysses on his birthday

Gabriel's new family: Raphael, Sylphide, and Ulysses

The other animals were intensely interested in this new little being, but I was keeping them separate so Sylphide could relax and recuperate after the birth and not have to worry about protecting him. I did not try to approach the baby, but when he tripped over to me on his little feet, his mother left her food and inserted herself between us. I told her I wouldn't try to touch him and she let me stay nearby.

Father and son

As I was walking back to the house after the animals and I watched the baby donkey for what, in my case, might have been hours—the other animals soon returned to eating—I counted on my fingers again. Donkey gestation is about a year. The numbers didn't seem to compute, given Sylphide's consistent size. I gave up trying to figure it out. It was Gabriel's journey. Then I remembered his visit to my dreams after he had died—the two donkeys, and then the third, who curled up in my lap and went to sleep. Gabriel had told me then that his family would arrive, and here they were. Gabriel was starting a new journey. Then the baby's name came to me: Ulysses.

This seeker would lead us we knew not where.

Flowing with Change

Whatever life events we encounter—beginnings, endings, a birth or a death—we walk the Way of Change. The Way of Change is about flowing with change, but that doesn't mean just sitting back and waiting for life to happen. Instead, we take part in creating the changes that arrive in our lives.

I rescued two donkeys, or the universe and Gabriel helped create the circumstances in which I could step up and act on behalf of donkeys in need. For me, the term "cocreation" best expresses the changes that emerge in our lives as a result of the connections between multiple beings, here and in the beyond. As cocreators, the choices we make have everything to do with how the cocreation turns out.

If I had not called the phone number, Sylphide, Raphael, and Ulysses would not be with me. If I had not established a relationship with Bud and shown him that I was serious by arranging a trailer and trying to get the donkeys, he would probably not have bothered calling about the two he caught. If I hadn't listened to Gabriel, none of it would have happened. Cocreation depends on the active participation of all the cocreators.

As with any creation, change is integral to cocreation. A creation cannot occur without change. The animals regularly show me what the natural human reaction to change would be if we let ourselves have it. We are, after all, animals, too. Animals don't like change. Change requires adjustment. They would prefer that things stay the same. And even when the environment they know is bad, animals don't embrace the unknown. After all, it could be even worse! If we humans would let ourselves go with our natural impulses, we would acknowledge that we, like the rest of the animals, don't like change. Like them, it could take us months to adjust to a new situation, even when the change is a positive, exciting one.

Sylphide and Raphael cried or ranted or lamented or commented vociferously, however you want to interpret their braying, for two days. They let themselves express whatever they needed to express about their change in circumstances. Then they could begin to be present to interact with their new surroundings. They did not leap into the new but proceeded with judiciousness. It struck me as a shining example of self-respect and self-love; these two knew how to care for themselves.

Likewise, Pegasus did not jump forward and embrace these strangers as her new best friends. She hung back to observe and consider, and then she let their relationship unfold slowly as they all got to know each other. The sheep did the same. Rarely do we meet a soul mate, and we suffer when we try to create one out of someone who isn't.

The animals know how to forge deep and lasting relationships that are built on reality, not on fiction. They know how to flow with change; part of that is to acknowledge that change requires adjustment and it is fine to take your time. They know how to flow with change, but they also know how to be consistent. And they let each other know when they don't like something. They don't just passively accept everything that comes along. When a tarp blows off the roof, they spook.

We can use that as a metaphor. Ever since someone from the West brought the great news to the rest of the West that the elements of the Chinese character for "crisis"

can be translated as "crisis equals opportunity," we have been plagued with the idea that we're supposed to embrace life's awful events as a chance to grow and evolve. Although it can be true that the challenges of life make us bigger people, that doesn't mean we aren't allowed to respond naturally to changes, that is, to spook at the tarp blowing off the roof, or rant and lament like Sylphide and Raphael. In the Western tendency to reduce the complex to the simplistic, much was lost in the translation of the Chinese character. An accurate translation is not the three-word formula. Though there is still much more to be said to render an accurate translation, the upshot is that crisis and danger tell us only that things could go either way: we could get tangled in the tarp and break a leg, or the tarp could blow harmlessly away.

Flowing with change means acknowledging that change requires some adjustment. If we run around for months talking about the scary tarp that blew away, we might have yet to recognize the truism that "feelings are just feelings." Sylphide and Raphael didn't pull out their hair and keen and wail for weeks. They gave it what it needed and moved on. Pegasus and the sheep did the same.

When we love ourselves unconditionally, we give ourselves the space and time we need to adjust to life events and other shifts in circumstances. But we also each have a responsibility not to inflict our personal sackcloths on others. When we allow ourselves to experience our true reaction to change, we are less likely to prolong our reaction or dramatize it.

When we love others unconditionally, we accept their reactions, needs, and time frame in dealing with change. We don't expect them to conform to our way of reacting, nor do we hold them to what we think is the right amount of time to adjust. As with grief, the time line depends on the individual.

If we look to animals as our teachers in Flowing with Change, we see that animals who have been abused require more time for adjustment when change occurs. If they receive consistent and ongoing unconditional love from the beings who show up and stay present in their lives, that adjustment time may be shortened. Healthy animals do not pretend that a change is not upsetting, but they react to it as they need to and then move on when they have fully processed the change. Again, communication from their humans as to what is happening, along with loving reassurance, can shorten that time.

Flowing with change means providing that same loving support to ourselves and to each other. The Way of Change tells us that what is truly embedded in crisis is the opportunity to love each other more.

10

Sanctuary

A MESSENGER ARRIVED IN AN UNEXPECTED FORM. I was attending a Mystical Activism on Behalf of Animals conference in the northern California town of Shasta, in the shadow of the sacred mountain. The directors of an elephant sanctuary were also there and told of what is done to elephants to "train" them. We've all heard enough animal cruelty stories, so I won't go into the details aside from saying that the trainers beat the elephants with two-by-fours. Images of cruelty stay in my mind. On this day, I was particularly haunted; I couldn't lose the sickness I felt when I heard about the abuse of these noble beings. At the end of the day, I sought the comfort of nature, hiking up Mount Shasta.

The family

Chloe in the dandelions

I prayed to the mountain spirits for guidance as I walked up the road past the gate that closes the summit to cars in the winter because of the snow. Tall pine trees, with snowbanks at their feet, lined both sides of the road. Though the sun shone brightly, the air still held the chill of winter. I walked, taking in some of the beauty, but the images of the elephants being beaten kept replaying in my head and I was crying. The director had said the trainers "love" their elephants. "How could they treat them that way?" I asked the sacred mountain. My question expanded to, "How can people do all the awful things they do to each other and to animals?"

As I climbed higher, still weeping, I began to try to feel compassion for the trainers and everyone else who resorted to violence. People who abused animals and children, and leaders who dropped bombs on other countries, were always a huge challenge for me in this practice.

I suddenly remembered the old housetraining practice of hitting a puppy with a newspaper after the puppy had peed on the floor. You were supposed to push the puppy's nose into the urine, even if it was a long time later, and then whack the puppy with a newspaper. Most of the time, the poor puppy had no idea what this punishment was about, and it was likely to result in a dog that cringes, a "cowed" dog. My family loved animals and yet this is what we did, because it was the approved practice. As a teenager, I did this with my new puppy. Granted, I didn't hit him hard, but I unquestioningly inflicted my superior size and strength on him through the nose-pushing and the news-paper-whacking. He cowered. I think I only did it once, not being able to stand the cringing. Nevertheless, tender-hearted as I was, I had done it.

On the sacred mountain, I received an answer to my aching questions. It's a continuum—a continuum of violence and a continuum of consciousness. I loved the puppy, yet I struck him, even if only with a newspaper. The violence of the elephant trainers was hardly compara-ble in the pain it inflicted, but the trainers and I were both inflicting fear and neither of us questioned this accepted practice, even though we "loved" our animals. If we had been fully in touch with our hearts, we wouldn't have done what we did.

As I stood above the tree line on the snowy sacred peak, I was humbled. I could no longer separate myself from the elephant trainers—an extremely unwelcome realization, to say the least. I wanted to view us as diametrically differ-ent, but the memory of the puppy told me the difference between us was only a matter of degree. All I could say was that I had realized the error of my ways and was doing my best to live with an open heart. Perhaps the trainers were, too. In our violent culture, we are all somewhere on the continuum of violence until we consciously strive to step away from it. We are all also on the continuum of consciousness, wherever we are in our soul learning. Some of us may have learned a lot already, but we all still have much to learn.

As I walked back down the mountain, I felt sad and uplifted at the same time. Saddened by the damage we humans, including me, inflict in our ignorance and unconsciousness. Uplifted by a renewed sense of connection and clarity. I gave thanks to the elephants and the sacred mountain spirits for bearing their messages to me.

I saw that the continuum of consciousness is a continuum of love. Consciousness expands as the heart opens. We are all apprentices on the continuum of love. When we step onto that path, we apprentice ourselves to animals, to each other, to nature, to the universe. We are learning to open our hearts more completely to another, whether that other is an animal, a person, a tree, or a flower.

As you integrate the lessons of unconditional love, your heart opens and one day you find you are in the flow of the universe. You look into the eyes of a cat and suddenly you feel the oneness that is always there, waiting for you, and you know with your deepest knowing that you are part of the universal whole. You know you are not alone and never will be. You know we are all connected.

We can tap into that connection simply by asking, "What can I do today to open my heart?" For the animals in your life, ask yourself, "Are there ways I can allow them to live truer to their natures? Are there things I can do to accommodate their true selves that I am not doing because it might be inconvenient for me? What can I do today to open my heart?"

Ulysses

You might not think you have obstacles to opening your heart, but we all do to one degree or another. When it comes to animals, maybe you have the belief that you shouldn't love an animal as much as you do, telling yourself, "It's just a dog." Our culture is beginning to catch up with the reality of people's deep attachment to animals, but the old training that we should not care too much persists. For instance, a beloved animal's death is not accepted as akin to the loss of human loved ones. Many people feel ashamed and try to hide their grief over the loss of an animal family member. Many of us have internalized the view that "It's only an animal."

Denial of our inherent connection and outright ridicule of those who show a passionate connection with nature have been elements of society since the Goddess was removed from human spirituality. In the fifth millennium BCE, men on horseback thundered down from the steppes of northern Europe and overthrew the peaceable agrarian peoples who respected and revered the divine feminine. Her temples have been under siege ever since, as have women and nature. A passionate connection to nature is a subversive act because it threatens the structures of a society invested in exploiting it. Isn't it wonderful that in doing something so joyful as hugging a tree or a sheep we are committing an act of rebellion?

A herd of horses and I recently reclaimed ancient ritual. As I'm sure was the case with the rituals of yore, it all arose organically. I had come to a horse sanctuary to do energy healing work with Toby, a twelve-year-old dark bay thoroughbred, to help him recover from his horrific past. Toby now lived in the wide-open space of connecting pastures with a friendly herd of horses, but he ignored them, except for Tuli, the chestnut mare who had become his constant companion. He had taught her an addictive behavior called cribbing and they spent most of the day and night at the fence doing this, despite the beautiful land to roam.

Cribbing, also known as wind sucking, is a serious problem, typically among horses who are being kept or have been kept in stalls most of the time. They grip the wooden edge of the stall or fence and pull back while sucking in air to send a rush of dopamine to their brains, which gives them a momentary feeling of elation. Toby had not been kept in a stall since arriving on the sanctuary three years before, yet he could not let go of the behavior that had gotten him through terrible times. His former person, who purportedly "loved" him, lived a roving lifestyle and often left him for long periods, not only confined in a stall but without food. He endured starvation and a winter spent knee deep in mud. Like Gabriel, he had left his body. I could see this when I met him. He didn't seem to see me, his eyes passing over me as if I weren't there. The cribbing, as with any addiction, was self-medication. What else could a horse with no escape from horror do?

In my energy work with Toby, I first focused on helping him release the trauma from his past so he could come back into his body and begin to live his beautiful present. He seemed to be enjoying the work, which is noninvasive. But when I said, "Toby, you can let go of the past," suddenly, without warning (such as ears pinning back), he lowered his head to my stomach and bit me hard. In thinking about it later, I got the sense that Toby hadn't realized he could walk away, though we were standing in a pasture and he was under no restraint. In his mind, he was still in that stall where he had been trapped for so many years. How could he let go of the past when he was still living it? If I wanted to put a label on his mental state, I could say "post-traumatic stress disorder." He could not stop reliving his past.

Raphael

In my sessions with him after that, I kept a respectful distance instead of crowding him in his stall, so to speak. As I worked to restore balance to his energy field, which would improve the function of all his body systems and trigger his innate ability to heal himself, I began sending him messages: You are strong. You are home. You are safe. You can open your heart and still keep yourself safe.

Sanctuary staff commented on a change in Toby. One day they saw him lying down taking a nap in the sun, which no one had seen him do before. Was he beginning to come home?

At the next session, I was inspired to try distracting Toby from his cribbing with other activities. Horses, it is said, see the pictures in your head. The rest of the herd was at the top of the hill, in the eucalyptus grove, while Toby and Tuli were cribbing at the fence below as usual. I visualized us taking a walk together and Toby and Tuli joining the herd. I took a few steps up the slope. Moments later, Toby left the fence, with Tuli following, and we began a meandering walk up the hill. When he stopped, I was guided to sing to him. The song that came to me was a variation on a Gaia circle song:

> Isis, Astarte, Diana, Hecate,
> Demeter, Kali
> Inanna
>
> I am a strong horse
> I am a story horse
> I am a healer
> My soul will never die

When I sang, he moved toward me. Then he would graze. Then I would sing. In this way, I sang him up the hill, with words sung to the same tune emerging from me, carrying healing messages for him. As we neared the top, I said, "You lead the way, Toby," and he did—all the way to the eucalyptus trees where he took his place at the edge of the herd. I moved farther into the shade among the horses and he came to me, fully present. I stroked him and did some energy work while telling him that he is the only one who can make himself feel safe, but all the other horses and the people on the sanctuary who love him are there to help.

When I finished, I sat down under a tree and sang to the whole herd.

> We are strong horses
> We are story horses
> We are healers
> Our souls will never die
>
> Isis, Astarte, Diana, Hecate,
> Demeter, Kali
> Inanna
>
> We are old horses
> We are new horses
> We are the same horses
> deeper than before

I continued singing and, again, words emerged with affirming messages for the horses. All of them, including Toby and Tuli, drowsed with drooping eyelids, serene, together, content.

When I walked back down the hill, Toby and Tuli did not follow me. When I drove away, they were still up there. My heart thrilled to see those who had so often separated themselves being part of the herd.

Sylphide and Ulysses

Two weeks later, the horses graced me with another transportive experience. I treated Tuli first because she seemed to be in need. When I went to Toby, he was ready to receive me. I did some energy work with the same message: You are safe. You are home. You are strong.

Then I began singing. The other horses moved in and formed a circle. The wise elder of the group stood with his nose close to Toby's flank and the little mare who is his constant companion stood with her nose at her friend's flank, with another mare filling the space between the little mare and me, with me next to Toby. Tuli and two of the others stood on the outside of the circle but were just as much a part of it. No one left and Toby cribbed only briefly once or twice during this long singing circle, which was right by the fence where he could crib whenever he wanted.

The song that emerged was a horse healing song that told them they are healers because of all they've been through, that their stories can help heal others, that we can all help each other heal, we are home, we are one, we are a circle, a circle of love. I sang to them for a long time and it was as though we were all in a meditative trance together. I envisioned the healing rippling out from us in waves, traveling to those who needed it.

> We are strong elephants
> We are story elephants
> We are healers
> Our souls will never die

UNCONDITIONAL LOVE LESSON #10:
Every Moment Is a Sanctuary

The heart of the healer is a four-chambered heart, says Angeles Arrien. It is not enough to have an *open* heart. For health and healing in all realms of body, mind, and spirit, the heart must be *full, clear,* and *strong* as well.

My heart gives a leap of joy when I greet an animal. My heart jumps in joy to meet the heart of that animal. I feel my four-chambered heart open, full, clear, and strong. It could not be that way if the animals had not taught me how to create a sanctuary within. With an inner sanctuary, my sight is the vision of my heart, which, heedless of accepted practice, guides me to ever more openness, strength, fullness, and clarity.

With an inner sanctuary, we welcome ourselves home in each moment of our lives. With an inner sanctuary, we can create sanctuary everywhere we go.

The Animal Messenger teachings revealed to me the true meaning of sanctuary: a place to feel safe, a place where one can be completely oneself, a place of supported independence, a place to live and die in peace, a place of deep connection on a heart and spirit level, a place of love, honor, and respect for all beings.

With an open, strong, full, and clear heart, we can create sanctuary in every moment of our lives. Welcoming each moment, we walk the Way of Welcome and extend sanctuary to everyone we meet, offering a place of peace even in a passing interaction.

You might think it is exhausting to walk through your days bringing love to every moment, but it is actually energizing. What saps our energy is the energy it takes to try to ignore the pain of the world and to shut off the connection that is our natural way. If we meet the world with love in our hearts—and a silent communication of caring takes only a second—we return home feeling stronger from the moments of acknowledgment that we are all connected.

Trinity

In the Way of Welcome, in the unconditional love of the full, open, clear, and strong heart, we bring love and respect to all our relationships. A traditional Lakota Sioux prayer begins "Mitakuye Oyasin," translated variously as "All my relations" or "All my relatives" or "We are all related," an acknowledgment that all elements of the natural world are connected, that every tree, rock, plant, animal, person, insect, bird, frog, snake, and so on is our relation. In passing each heated stone into the sweat lodge for sacred ceremony, the fire keeper says, "Mitakuye Oyasin," in recognition of the stone people. Those praying in the lodge often begin and end their prayer with the phrase, honoring all our relations and the oneness of all. Some people use it as a sign-off in letters and emails. I say it in thanks to the moment because, when I am welcoming the moment, I am feeling one with all creation. "Aho Mitakuye Oyasin," I say, in gratitude for the beautiful world around me and for the joy of living life with the Animal Messengers.

All my relations.

12 Things

You Can Do to Help the Animal Messengers

1. Consider your relationship with the animals in your life. Ask yourself whether you are exerting control or honoring and respecting who each is. Answer the same question regarding the people in your life, nature, and yourself. Are you honoring and respecting all?

2. Educate yourself on the state of the environment and the plight of animal species.

3. Practice harm reduction. Eat low on the food chain. If you eat animal products, consider eating only meat, dairy, or eggs from free-range animals and birds, organically raised if possible (with neither growth hormone to boost milk production nor constant antibiotic use), and avoid entirely veal, pâté de foie gras, and factory-raised pork (the practices used against calves, geese, and pigs to produce these foods are particularly horrible).

4. Conserve resources: reduce, reuse, recycle. Avoid buying products with excessive packaging. Save electricity and water; turn the lights out when you exit a room and turn the tap off while you are brushing your teeth, washing a dish, soaping your hands at the sink, or shampooing your hair in the shower. Drive a fuel-efficient vehicle and carpool, take public transportation, bicycle, or walk when you can.

5. Support environmental causes and organizations working for the benefit of nature and animals.

6. Use nontoxic household and garden products. Use natural shampoo, soap, and other body products. All pesticides and chemicals you use in your house or garden end up in the water table.

7. Support companies that do not test on animals, and do not buy products from those that do.

8. Spend time in nature, every day if possible, even if it is just smelling a flower or stopping to appreciate a tree on a city street. Give thanks to the natural world around you for all it provides.

9. Acknowledge the people you encounter as you move through your day. Do not treat the people who serve you in stores or other businesses as if they are not there. Let them know that you see them, by acknowledging them with a smile and a thank-you.

10. Every being in the world, every aspect of nature, is your neighbor. Love all thy neighbors and thyself.

11. Consider what you are contributing to the world and ask yourself what else you can do to make the world a better place.

12. Remember that you, too, are a Messenger and can create sanctuary everywhere you go and in everything you do.

Acknowledgments

My deepest thanks to:

All the animals who have graced my life. I am eternally grateful.

All the wonderful people who have generously helped the sanctuary and me. The animals and I thank you!

Everyone at Red Wheel/Weiser/Conari/Hampton Roads for all your efforts on behalf of this book.

Special thanks to Greg Brandenburgh and Caroline Pincus for your vision in bringing this book to the wide world, and to Jim Warner for your beautiful cover design, which makes me smile every time I look at it.

My beloved friends, treasured family, and all my guides for who you are and the blessing of you in my life.